PHILIP'S

Cycle TOURS

Kent and Sussex

Nick Cotton

First published in 2002 by
Philip's, a division of
Octopus Publishing Group Ltd
2-4 Heron Quays
London E14 4JP

First edition 2002
First impression 2002

Based on the original Ordnance Survey Cycle Tours series
first published by Philip's and Ordnance Survey®.

ISBN 0-540-08194-9

The route maps in this book are reproduced from
Ordnance Survey® Landranger® mapping.

Text and compilation copyright © Philip's 2002

Ordnance Survey®

This product includes mapping data licensed from Ordnance
Survey® with the permission of the Controller of Her Majesty's
Stationery Office. © Crown copyright 2002. All rights reserved.
Licence number 100011710

Photographic acknowledgements

AA Photo Library 37, 89 • Nick Cotton 85, 109, 121 • Reed
International Books (Adam Woolfit) 95 • Judy Todd 31 top •
Graham Todd 67 • Andy Williams 25, 31, 49, 55

Contents

On-road routes

1 Midhurst to Petersfield and back along the foot of the South Downs   6

2 Rolling woodland northeast of Midhurst   12

3 Chichester and the South Downs   18

4 Ruined castles, Roman villas and rough riding west and north of Storrington   24

5 South from Balcombe to the South Downs below Ditchling Beacon   30

6 Between Ashdown Forest and the South Downs near Uckfield   36

7 From Hailsham across the Pevensey Levels and over the Sussex Weald   42

8 Through the eastern reaches of the Weald, north and east of Battle   48

9 South from Tenterden to Rye   54

10 Tenterden to Sissinghurst Castle   60

11 Wye to Chilham   66

12 Narrow lanes and extensive views on the eastern end of the North Downs   72

13 Sandwich and quiet Kent villages in the southeastern corner of England   78

Off-road routes

1 Along the Greensand Way south of Godalming   84

2 From Buriton onto the western end of the South Downs   88

3 Glorious downland riding near Goodwood   92

4 West from Amberley on the South Downs Way over Bignor Hill to East Dean   96

5 East from Amberley over Wepham Down and Rackham Hill   100

6 North of Worthing: Cissbury Ring to the Adur Valley and Chanctonbury   104

7 West from Alfriston over the Downs to Firle Beacon   108

8 East from Alfriston via Friston Forest to Jevington and Windover Hill   112

9 From Wye onto the North Downs to northeast of Ashford   116

10 On the North Downs above the Elham Valley, north of Folkestone   120

11 Behind the White Cliffs: the North Downs near Dover   124

Abbreviations and symbols

Directions

L	left
R	right
LH	left-hand
RH	right-hand
SA	straight ahead or straight across
T-j	T-junction, a junction where you have to give way
X-roads	crossroads, a junction where you may or may not have to give way
'Placename 2'	words in quotation marks are those that appear on signposts; the numbers indicate distance in miles unless stated otherwise

Distance and grade

The number of drink bottles indicates the grade:

Easy

Moderate

Strenuous

The grade is based on the amount of climbing involved.

Refreshments

Pubs and teashops on or near the route are listed. The tankard ❦ symbols indicate pubs particularly liked by the author.

Page diagrams

The page diagrams on the introductory pages show how the map pages have been laid out, how they overlap and if any inset maps have been used.

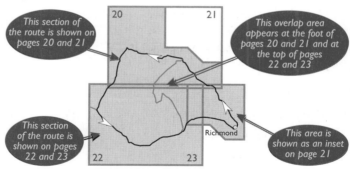

This section of the route is shown on pages 20 and 21

This overlap area appears at the foot of pages 20 and 21 and at the top of pages 22 and 23

This section of the route is shown on pages 22 and 23

This area is shown as an inset on page 21

Richmond

20 21 22 23

Cross-profiles

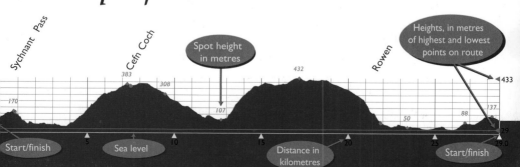

Sychnant Pass

Cefn Coch

Spot height in metres

Rowen

Heights, in metres of highest and lowest points on route

383

308

432

433

170

107

137

50

88

29

Start/finish

Sea level

Distance in kilometres

Start/finish

5 10 15 20 25 29.0

Legend to 1:50 000 maps

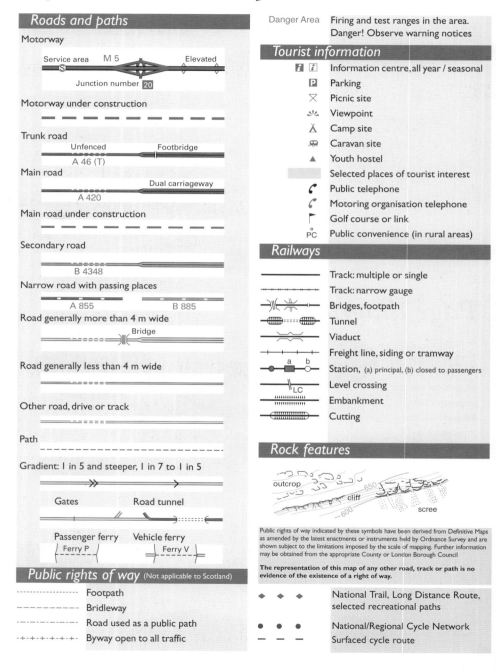

Roads and paths

Motorway

Service area M 5 Elevated
S
Junction number 20

Motorway under construction

Trunk road

Unfenced Footbridge
A 46 (T)

Main road

Dual carriageway
A 420

Main road under construction

Secondary road

B 4348

Narrow road with passing places

A 855 B 885

Road generally more than 4 m wide

Bridge

Road generally less than 4 m wide

Other road, drive or track

Path

Gradient: 1 in 5 and steeper, 1 in 7 to 1 in 5

Gates Road tunnel

Passenger ferry Vehicle ferry
Ferry P Ferry V

Public rights of way (Not applicable to Scotland)

.... Footpath
— — — — — Bridleway
—·—·—·— Road used as a public path
-+-+-+-+-+- Byway open to all traffic

Danger Area | Firing and test ranges in the area. Danger! Observe warning notices

Tourist information

🄸	ⓘ	Information centre, all year / seasonal
	P	Parking
	✕	Picnic site
	🔆	Viewpoint
	⅄	Camp site
	⛟	Caravan site
	▲	Youth hostel
	▨	Selected places of tourist interest
	✆	Public telephone
	✆	Motoring organisation telephone
	Γ	Golf course or link
	PC	Public convenience (in rural areas)

Railways

——————— Track: multiple or single
—++++——++++— Track: narrow gauge
Bridges, footpath
Tunnel
Viaduct
—+—+—+—+— Freight line, siding or tramway
a b
Station, (a) principal, (b) closed to passengers
LC Level crossing
Embankment
Cutting

Rock features

outcrop 650
cliff
600 scree

Public rights of way indicated by these symbols have been derived from Definitive Maps as amended by the latest enactments or instruments held by Ordnance Survey and are shown subject to the limitations imposed by the scale of mapping. Further information may be obtained from the appropriate County or London Borough Council

The representation of this map of any other road, track or path is no evidence of the existence of a right of way.

◆ ◆ ◆ | National Trail, Long Distance Route, selected recreational paths

● ● ● | National/Regional Cycle Network
— — — | Surfaced cycle route

Water features

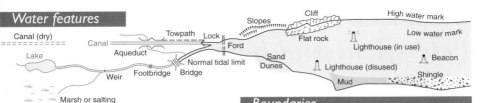

Canal (dry)
Canal
Aqueduct
Lake
Weir Footbridge Bridge
Towpath Lock
Ford
Normal tidal limit
Marsh or salting
Slopes Cliff High water mark
Flat rock Low water mark
Lighthouse (in use)
Sand Beacon
Dunes Lighthouse (disused)
Mud Shingle

General features

Electricity transmission line (with pylons spaced conventionally)

Pipeline (arrow indicates direction of flow)

Buildings

Public buildings (selected)

Bus or coach station

Coniferous wood

Non-coniferous wood

Mixed wood

Orchard

Park or ornamental grounds

Quarry

Spoil heap, refuse tip or dump

Radio or TV mast

Church or chapel with tower

Church or chapel with spire

Church or chapel without tower or spire

Chimney or tower

Glasshouse

Graticule intersection at 5' intervals

Heliport

Triangulation pillar

Windmill with or without sails

Windpump

Boundaries

National

London borough

National park or forest park

NT National Trust
    NT open access
    NT limited access

County, region or islands area

District

Abbreviations

P   Post office
PH   Public house
MS   Milestone
MP   Milepost
CH   Clubhouse
PC   Public convenience (in rural areas)
TH   Town hall, guildhall or equivalent
CG   Coastguard

Antiquities

VILLA   Roman

Castle   Non-Roman

Battlefield (with date)

Tumulus

Position of antiquity which cannot be drawn to scale

Ancient monuments and historic buildings in the care of the Secretaries of State for the Environment, for Scotland and for Wales and that are open to the public

Heights

50   Contours are at 10 metres vertical interval

·144   Heights are to the nearest metre above mean sea level

Heights shown close to a triangulation pillar refer to the station height at ground level and not necessarily to the summit

Midhurst to Petersfield and back along the foot of the South Downs

The route leaves the valley of the River Rother, taking some impressive sunken lanes through woods north to Milland. It is worth stopping there to look at the beautiful work produced by The Living Tree, including wooden toys from all over the world. The ride climbs to cross the A3 at Hill Brow and sweeps down through Liss to come around the back of Petersfield. Around the large square in Petersfield, there are many watering holes and attractive Georgian houses. Having left the B2146 at Nursted, the ride is an absolute dream of quiet flat lanes beneath the folds of the South Downs back to Midhurst.

Start

The Silver Shoe PH, High St, Midhurst

P Heading north out of town on the A286

Distance and grade

45 km (28 miles)
Moderate

Terrain

Three climbs: 91 m (300 ft)between Midhurst and Milland, 91 m (300 ft) from Milland to Hill Brow on the A3, 79 m (260 ft) from Liss to Bushy Hill. Flat from Petersfield back to Midhurst

Nearest railway

Petersfield

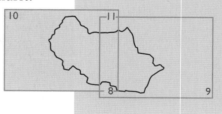

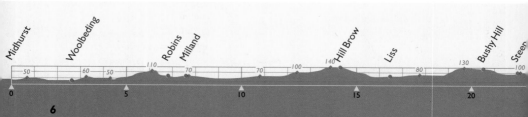

Places of interest

Midhurst 1

The origins of this town lie in the early Middle Ages when the Norman Lord, Savaric Fitzcane, built a castle on St Anne's Hill. This castle is now completely ruined but there are many other buildings that display Midhurst's history.

Midhurst Parish Church

This church and its beautiful churchyard overlook the Market Square

Market Hall, Town Hall and The Spread Eagle

The timber building in front of the Spread Eagle is the 16th-century Market Hall where the Grammar School was founded in 1672. The Town Hall dates from the early 19th century and still has the stocks and lock up. The Spread Eagle is one of the most impressive buildings in the town.

Petersfield 16

Once an important town for the wool trade, Petersfield is now a busy market town. A statue of William III guards the central square and there is a large lake southeast of the town.

Refreshments

Spread Eagle PH 🍺🍺, lots of choice, **Midhurst**
Rising Sun PH, **Milland**
Crossing Gate PH, **Liss**
Drovers PH, **Hill Brow**
Cricketers PH 🍺, Harrow PH 🍺🍺, **Steep**
Lots of choice in **Petersfield**
White Hart PH 🍺, The Ship PH, Coach and Horses PH 🍺, **South Harting**
Three Horseshoes PH 🍺🍺, **Elsted**

Petersfield Nursted Quebec Elsted Treyford Bepton

80 80 90 90 80 80 90 80 60 140 30
25 30 35 40 45

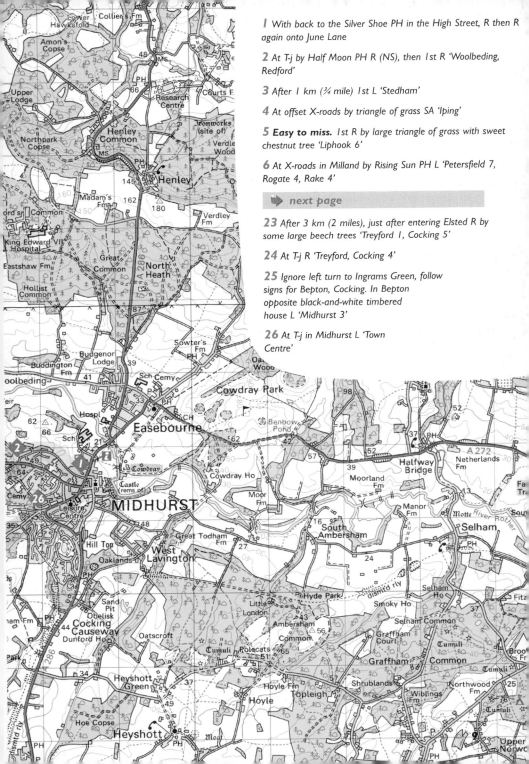

1 With back to the Silver Shoe PH in the High Street, R then R again onto June Lane

2 At T-j by Half Moon PH R (NS), then 1st R 'Woolbeding, Redford'

3 After 1 km (¾ mile) 1st L 'Stedham'

4 At offset X-roads by triangle of grass SA 'Iping'

5 **Easy to miss.** 1st R by large triangle of grass with sweet chestnut tree 'Liphook 6'

6 At X-roads in Milland by Rising Sun PH L 'Petersfield 7, Rogate 4, Rake 4'

▶ next page

23 After 3 km (2 miles), just after entering Elsted R by some large beech trees 'Treyford 1, Cocking 5'

24 At T-j R 'Treyford, Cocking 4'

25 Ignore left turn to Ingrams Green, follow signs for Bepton, Cocking. In Bepton opposite black-and-white timbered house L 'Midhurst 3'

26 At T-j in Midhurst L 'Town Centre'

7 Continue on this road for 5 km (3 miles) following signs for Petersfield through X-roads at the top of hill

8 At T-j R uphill 'Petersfield 3, Liss 1'

9 At offset X-roads with the B2070 by the Drovers PH, SA onto B3006 'Liss 1'

10 Through Liss, crossing railway line. At T-j with A325 R 'Farnham, Alton', then 1st L 'Hawkley 2, Priors Dean 3'

11 After 1½ km (1 mile) 1st L 'Wheatham, Steep Marsh'

12 Up steep hill. At T-j L 'Steep, Petersfield' and follow signs for Steep for 2½ km (1½ miles), ignoring left and right turns

13 Where Mill Lane ends at T-j R (NS)

14 At T-j by The Cricketers PH L 'Petersfield'

15 At roundabout L 'Town Centre, Midhurst 11'

16 After crossing railway lines 2nd R onto Chapel Street

17 At T-j at end of High Street by the war memorial R then after 300 m (yd) L by filling station onto Sussex Road 'South Harting B2146'

18 After almost 3 km (2 miles), shortly after going under power lines, on sharp RH bend L by triangle of grass (NS)

19 1st R 'West Harting'

20 At T-j R 'South Harting 2', then 1st L 'West Harting'

21 At T-j R 'South Harting'. At next T-j R 'South Harting'

22 At T-j in South Harting L 'Midhurst, Elsted'

23 After 3 km (2 miles), just after entering Elsted R by some large beech trees 'Treyford 1, Cocking 5'

◀ previous page

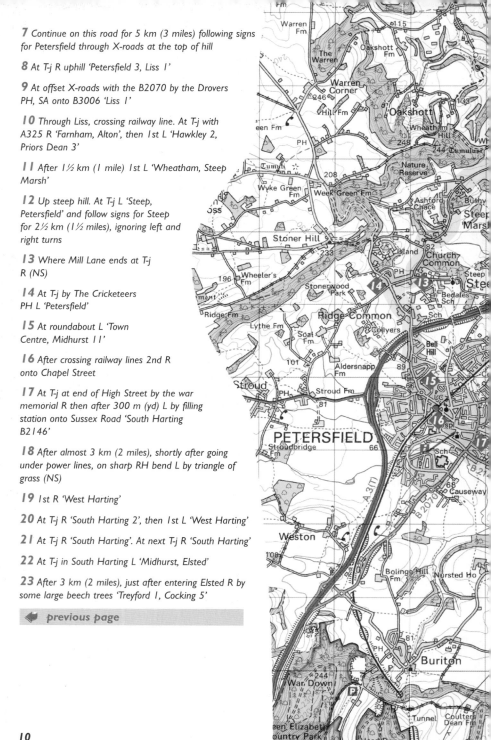

2 Rolling woodland northeast of Midhurst

There is easy cycling on quiet lanes north of the South Downs. This ride links the historic towns of Midhurst and Petworth via a loop through wooded lanes and small villages such as Lodsworth and Plaistow. There are many good pubs along the way and the chance of a tea stop in Petworth or back at Midhurst.

Refreshments

*Plenty of choice in **Midhurst** and **Petworth***
*Three Moles PH, **Selham***
*Stag Inn, **Balls Cross** Sun Inn, **Plaistow***
*Lickfold Inn ●●, **Lickfold***

Start

Knockhundred Road, by the building society in the centre of Midhurst

P Free long-term parking on the A286 Haslemere Road, going north out of Midhurst

Distance and grade

54 km (34 miles)
Easy/moderate

Terrain

In general, flat or undulating, but with two hills of 76 m (250 ft) in the first half of the ride, one from South Ambersham to the top of Leggatt Hill and one from Lickfold onto Shopp Hill

Nearest railway

Haslemere, 5 km (3 miles) from the route at Gospel Green, or Billingshurst, 10 km (6 miles) from the route at Kirdford

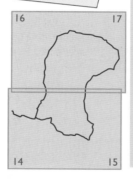

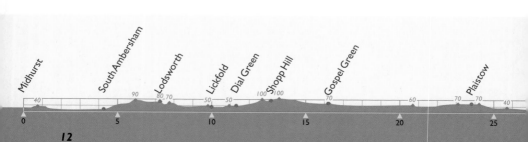

Cowdray House 2-3
Originally known as La Coudraye, this house was the residence of the de Bohun family when they left the castle at Midhurst. Construction began in 1530 and, despite a fire in 1793 that left the house a standing ruin, it is an impressive example of Tudor architecture.

Lodsworth 6 and Lickfold 7-8
These villages are typical of the area and are surrounded and bounded by streams and woods. Lodsworth has a charming collection of characterful houses and cottages.

Kirdford 13
A peaceful village with a 12th-century church and tiled cottages. In the 16th century, it was industrially important with forges and foundries, but this is now hard to believe.

Petworth House and Park 15-17
This magnificent house was built by Charles Seymour, 6th Duke of Somerset, in the late 17th century. Inside the house are some fascinating exhibitions and the North Gallery contains a very important collection of paintings, which includes works by Turner (who was a visitor here), Gainsborough and Van Dyke. The 700 acres of deer park were beautifully landscaped by `Capability' Brown.

Balls Cross

Gunter's Bridge

Petworth

Haslingbourne

Heath End

Selham

South Ambersham

30   50   60   30   20   30   40   30   40 30   40   100
                                                            10
30   35   40   45   50   55

1 Follow Knockhundred Road out of Midhurst and over the bridge

2 1st L after the bridge onto Selham Road 'West Lavington'

3 Ignore left turns on private road to Cowdray Park. After 3 km (2 miles), at triangle of grass 1st L (in effect SA) 'Lodsworth 2'

4 At T-j with A272 L 'Midhurst, Easebourne', then 1st R (NS). **Take care**

5 At T-j at top of hill bear L (NS)

6 At 'Lodsworth' sign 1st L on School Lane, then shortly afterwards L again, following School Lane

7 At T-j with Myrtle Cottage ahead L (NS)

 two pages

15 At T-j with A283 L (NS)

16 In Petworth, follow signs for Pulborough A283 until reaching X-roads

17 At X-roads with New Street SA onto Middle Street then at T-j after 100 m (yd) L onto High Street

18 At T-j at end of Grove Lane after almost 1½ km (1 mile) L 'Fittleworth'

19 1st R at X-roads, 'Sutton'

20 At X-roads R 'Duncton'

21 At T-j with A285 L 'Chichester 12, Duncton', then 1st R 'Selham 3 Graffham 3'

22 At T-j R 'Mihurst 5'. Just after Three Moles PH in Selham L 'South Ambersham, Midhurst'

23 At T-j R 'Midhurst 3, Lodsworth 3'

24 At triangle of grass L 'West Lavington 1, Midhurst 3'

25 Follow outward route back to start, turning R at T-j to cross bridge back into the centre of Midhurst

8 Continue on this road for 9 km (5½ miles), following signs for Haslemere

9 At T-j in Gospel Green R 'Petworth 7, Northchapel 2, Chiddingfold 3'

10 At X-roads with A283 SA 'Plaistow 4'

11 At T-j R 'Plaistow, Kirdford 4, Loxwood 4'

12 Follow signs for Kirdford and Petworth

13 At T-j in Kirdford R 'Petworth'

14 Follow signs for Petworth

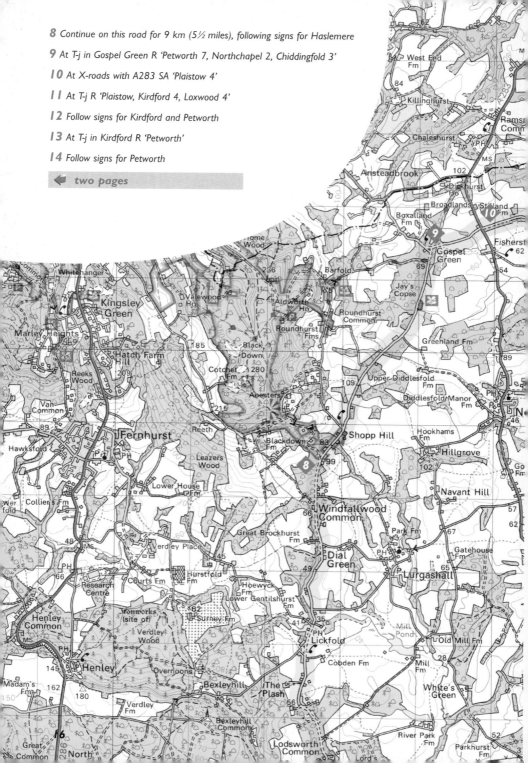

← **two pages**

3 *Chichester and the South Downs*

Starting in the striking old Roman town of Chichester, this ride avoids the busy roads to the east of Chichester by linking two no through roads via a short section of footpath, dropping you close to East Lavant. Goodwood House and Country Park are skirted to the east. The ride now meanders over the southwest section of the South Downs, passing through the attractive villages of East Dean, Charlton and Singleton, dropping to cross the River Lavant before climbing again towards Chilgrove and the Mardens. The return eastwards back to Chichester is easy, with two enticing detours possible, to Bosham and to Fishbourne Palace.

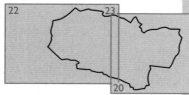

Start

The Cathedral shop by the Old Tower of Chichester Cathedral

P Follow signs in Chichester

Distance and grade

51 km (32 miles)
Easy/moderate

Terrain

The first half of the ride is undulating, the second half flat. A 91 m (300 ft) climb from Chichester over the downs to East Dean, then several shorter climbs of up to 61 m (200 ft), but nothing too serious.

Nearest railway

Chichester, or Rowland's Castle

Refreshments

Plenty of choice in **Chichester**
Hur dlemakers PH ♥, **East Dean**
The Fox PH ♥♥, **Charlton**
Fox and Hounds PH, **Singleton**
Selsey Arms PH, **West Dean**
The George PH, **Finchdean**
Several PHs in **Rowland's Castle**

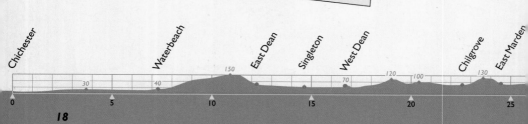

Chichester 1-3
This beautiful city with its cathedral and other fine buildings is a centre for both culture and history.

Chichester Cathedral 1
Built on the site of the shrine of St Richard, this cathedral was consecrated in 1184. It contains both Romanesque stone carvings and modern paintings, sculptures, tapestries and stained glass.

The Pallants 1-2
These four narrow streets are full of Georgian houses, Pallant House being the most impressive.

Market Cross 1-2
Chichester's four main streets were laid by the Romans and meet at the Market Cross, which was built by Bishop Story in 1501.

Goodwood House 6-7
Surrounded by parkland, this magnificent late 18th-century house contains beautiful French furniture, porcelain and an important art collection, which includes works by Canaletto, Reynolds, Stubbs and Van Dyck. The famous Goodwood racecourse is in the grounds.

Weald and Downland Open Air Museum, Singleton 9-10
This unusual museum, amidst beautiful Downland scenery, houses restored medieval farmsteads, barns and other agricultural buildings – even a 17th-century watermill in working order.

Stansted Park 21
This neo-Wren house was the home of the Earl and Countess of Bessborough. It was rebuilt in 1903 but has an ancient chapel, interesting exhibitions and a walled garden. There are wonderful views over the surrounding forest down to the English Channel.

Fishbourne Roman Palace and Museum 26-27
Fishbourne is the largest Roman residence to have been discovered in Britain. The underfloor heating systems and beautiful mosaic floors can be seen in the remains of the north wing. The gardens have also been restored to their Roman plan.

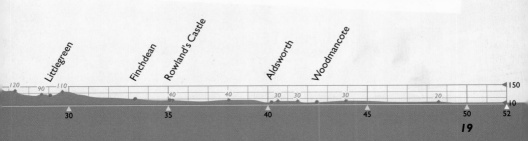

1 With your back to the tower SA onto Tower Street following one way system along Woolstaplers. At T-j at the end of Woolstaplers L 'Chapel St Car Park'

2 At T-j with North Walls R just before bridge (No Entry sign ahead). At T-j with North Street L. At roundabout R (**take care – use cycle lane**), following signs for 'Ring Road', 'Worthing (A27), Bognor (A259)'

3 At next roundabout SA, then 1st L opposite The Hope PH onto College Lane

4 Follow this road past hospital as it becomes Summersdale Road. 600 m (yd) after hospital, shortly after passing Highland Road to the left, turn R onto Fordwater Road

5 Go through 'No Through Road' sign. Road surface deteriorates. Shortly after crossing stream, before road turns sharply right towards house, L through small gate to follow stream. For the next 200 m (yd) this is a footpath, so get off and push your bike.

6 At T-j with New Road R. At 1st X-roads (Give Way) SA 'Halnaker, Petworth'. At next X-roads (your priority) L 'Goodwood Golf and Country Club'

7 Climb steadily for 3 km (2 miles). At X-roads SA 'East Dean 1'

8 In East Dean at T-j L 'Midhurst 8, Singleton 2'

9 In Singleton at triangle of grass L 'Chichester 6½'. At T-j with A286 L (NS). **Take care**

10 After 2 km (1¼ miles) at X-roads at the bottom of the hill by the Selsey Arms PH R '6ft 6ins width limit'

11 Ignore 1st L at brow of hill to Lodge Hill Farm. Descend the hill and take next L after 1 km (¾ mile) 'Chichester', then 1st R after 1 km (¾ mile) by oak and yew trees (sign vandalised)

12 At X-roads SA. At T-j with B2141 R 'Petersfield 9, Harting 5'

13 At top of hill, at exit of wood L 'East Marden, Stoughton 3'

➡ next page

26 Follow signs for Fishbourne. At X-roads SA onto Clay Lane 'Chichester'

27 At T-j L (NS). On sharp RH bend L 'Cyclists, Public Library, Council Offices'. Cross railway

28 At roundabout SA onto Westgate

29 At next roundabout SA onto West Street 'County Hall, Cathedral'

13 At top of hill, at exit of wood L 'East Marden, Stoughton 3'

14 In East Marden at thatched well R 'North Marden 1, Harting 4, Compton 3'

15 1st L 'Compton, Up Marden'. Follow up and over hill

16 At fork of roads R 'Harting 3'

17 At T-j with B2146, with oak tree ahead, R uphill (NS), then 1st L opposite Littlegreen School 'Finchdean 3'

18 At T-j L 'Finchdean'

19 At T-j R 'Rowland's Castle 1, Havant 4, Portsmouth 12'

20 After 1½ km (1 mile), just before going under railway bridge into Rowland's Castle L opposite the Castle Inn 'Stansted House'

21 At T-j L 'Westbourne 1, Funtington 3, Chichester 8'

22 At top of second short hill, with sign for Common Road on your left, R on Foxbury Lane 'Emsworth, Westbourne' and 1st L on Woodmancote Lane 'Woodmancote'

23 Through Woodmancote and past pub of same name. At T-j L then R onto West Ashling Road, following signs for the Ashlings

24 Just past a row of cream-coloured houses on the right (Edith Cottages) R on Southbrook Road by letter box (NS)

25 At T-j by triangle of grass R 'Bosham, Chichester'

previous page

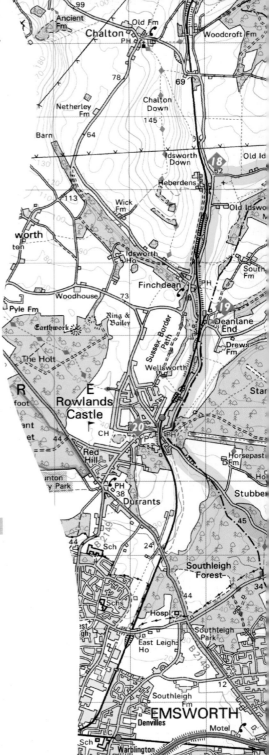

Ruined castles, Roman villas and rough riding west and north of Storrington

There are two points of interest in the early part of this varied ride: the ruined castle and the whole village of Amberley and the Roman villa at Bignor. Amberley, a delightful quiet backwater nestling beneath the South Downs, has many fine examples of houses built from a wide selection of materials. Bignor Roman Villa has the longest Roman mosaic on display in the country and you can see how the under-floor heating worked. The ride proceeds northwards and neatly avoids spending any time on the A283 by taking a rough but rideable track east of Byworth for a short distance. Passing through various stretches of woodland, the ride describes a loop around Billingshurst before returning to Storrington on quiet lanes.

Start

The White Horse Hotel in the centre of Storrington

P Near the library

Distance and grade

53 km (33 miles)
Easy/moderate

Terrain

Fairly flat or undulating. One climb of 100 m (330 ft) from Shopham Bridge over the River Rother south of Byworth to Flexham Park

Nearest railway

Amberley

Refreshments

Lots of choice in **Storrington**
The Sportsman PH 🍺, The Black Horse PH 🍺, Bridge PH 🍺, tea room, **Amberley**
George and Dragon PH 🍺🍺, **Houghton**
Black Dog and Duck PH 🍺, **Bury**
White Horse PH, **Sutton**
Black Horse PH 🍺🍺 (just off the route), Well Diggers PH, **Byworth**
Foresters PH 🍺, Half Moon PH 🍺, **Kirdford** (just off the route)
Well Diggers PH, **Byworth**
Cricketers Arms PH, **Wisborough Green** Bat and Ball Inn, **Newpound Common** Queens Head PH, **West Chiltington**

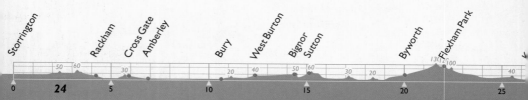

Parham House, Pulborough 3-4

Built in the late 16th century but with 18th-century additions, this grey stone, gabled house lies in an ancient deer park. The gardens were designed more recently and include walled gardens, a fountain and red water-lily pond and a temple garden. Inside the house are original carved panellings and Tudor and Jacobean furniture.

Amberley 6

An attractive village with twisting streets full of a variety of cottages, thatched, timbered, brick, stone and flint. The ruins of Amberley Castle, a former retreat of the Bishop of Chichester, and a Norman church stand on the edge of the village. The old Black Horse Inn is practically a museum with its collections of sheep bells and shepherds' crooks.

Amberley Chalk Pits Museum 6-7

This huge industrial museum is set in a 36-acre former chalk quarry with much of the original machinery on display. Other crafts and industries are demonstrated in workshops and visitors can travel around the area on the narrow gauge railway or the workmen's train.

▼ Mosaic floor at Bignor

Bignor 11

Some of the finest mosaic floors discovered outside Italy can be seen in the remains of this large Roman villa. The museum is also interesting and the surrounding countryside is beautiful.

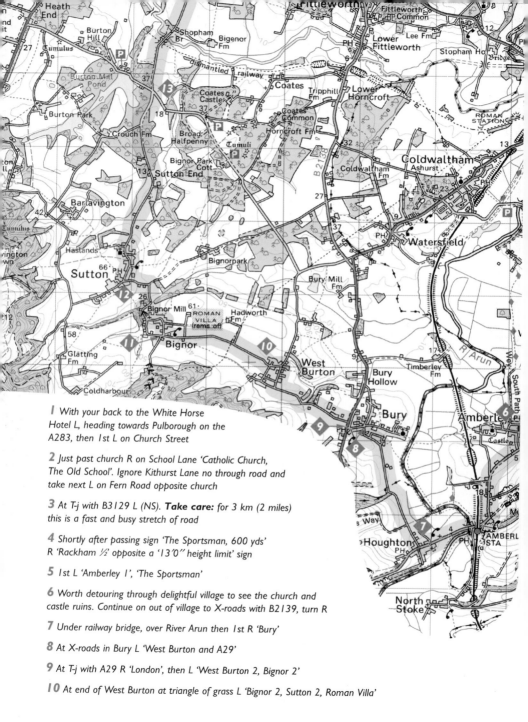

1 With your back to the White Horse Hotel L, heading towards Pulborough on the A283, then 1st L on Church Street

2 Just past church R on School Lane 'Catholic Church, The Old School'. Ignore Kithurst Lane no through road and take next L on Fern Road opposite church

3 At T-j with B3129 L (NS). **Take care:** for 3 km (2 miles) this is a fast and busy stretch of road

4 Shortly after passing sign 'The Sportsman, 600 yds' R 'Rackham ½' opposite a '13′0″ height limit' sign

5 1st L 'Amberley 1', 'The Sportsman'

6 Worth detouring through delightful village to see the church and castle ruins. Continue on out of village to X-roads with B2139, turn R

7 Under railway bridge, over River Arun then 1st R 'Bury'

8 At X-roads in Bury L 'West Burton and A29'

9 At T-j with A29 R 'London', then L 'West Burton 2, Bignor 2'

10 At end of West Burton at triangle of grass L 'Bignor 2, Sutton 2, Roman Villa'

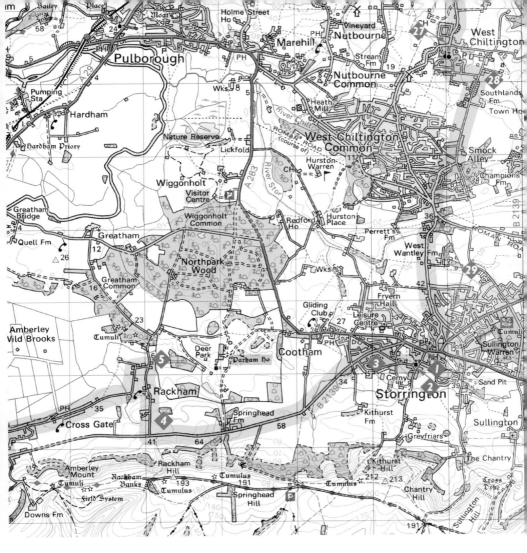

11 In Bignor follow signs for 'Sutton, Duncton'

12 At the White Horse PH in Sutton follow road uphill 'Byworth, Petworth'

13 At X-roads SA 'Petworth 3'

➡ *next page*

27 At X-roads in West Chiltington by Queens Head PH SA onto Church Street

28 At T-j R on Southlands Lane

29 This road becomes Smock Alley then Roundabout Lane and passes Five Bells PH. At T-j L (sign vandalised), then at T-j with B2139 R to return to Storrington

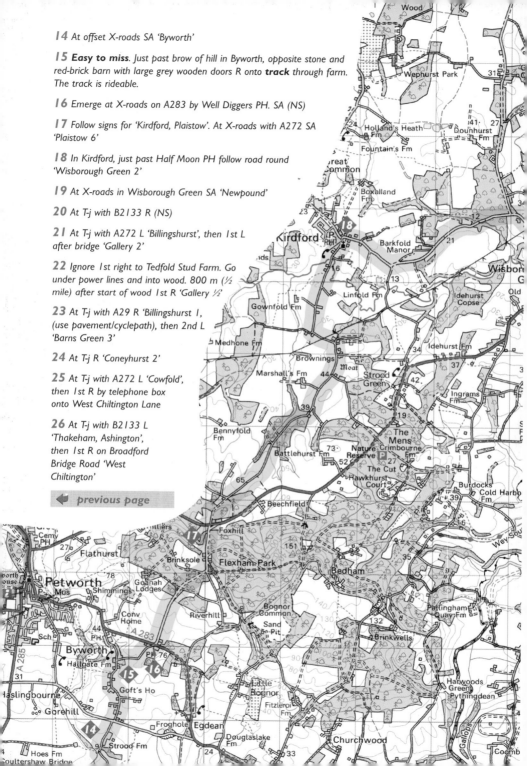

14 At offset X-roads SA 'Byworth'

15 **Easy to miss**. Just past brow of hill in Byworth, opposite stone and red-brick barn with large grey wooden doors R onto **track** through farm. The track is rideable.

16 Emerge at X-roads on A283 by Well Diggers PH. SA (NS)

17 Follow signs for 'Kirdford, Plaistow'. At X-roads with A272 SA 'Plaistow 6'

18 In Kirdford, just past Half Moon PH follow road round 'Wisborough Green 2'

19 At X-roads in Wisborough Green SA 'Newpound'

20 At T-j with B2133 R (NS)

21 At T-j with A272 L 'Billingshurst', then 1st L after bridge 'Gallery 2'

22 Ignore 1st right to Tedfold Stud Farm. Go under power lines and into wood. 800 m (½ mile) after start of wood 1st R 'Gallery ½'

23 At T-j with A29 R 'Billingshurst 1', (use pavement/cyclepath), then 2nd L 'Barns Green 3'

24 At T-j R 'Coneyhurst 2'

25 At T-j with A272 L 'Cowfold', then 1st R by telephone box onto West Chiltington Lane

26 At T-j with B2133 L 'Thakeham, Ashington', then 1st R on Broadford Bridge Road 'West Chiltington'

◀ previous page

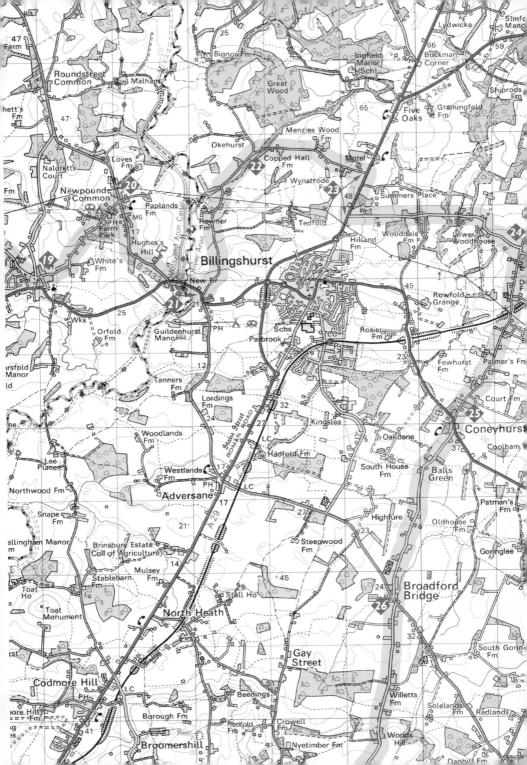

5 South from Balcombe to the South Downs below Ditchling Beacon

Balcombe is a small village north of Haywards Heath situated on the mainline railway from London and so a far easier starting point than Haywards Heath. Immediately into the heart of attractive Sussex countryside, the ride starts with fast descents and steep climbs either side of Ardingly Reservoir. Haywards Heath is skirted around and soon after crossing the A272, the South Downs appear on the horizon. The ride heads almost due south on quiet lanes, with views towards the steep chalk escarpment of the South Downs, rising to over 213 m (700 ft) at Ditchling Beacon. You are not asked to emulate the London to Brighton charity riders who climb up over Ditchling Beacon: content yourself with the views as you turn west along the foot of the hills to Clayton. After a crossing of the busy A273, more quiet lanes take you north past Hurstpierpoint College down into the Adur Valley before climbing back up to Balcombe.

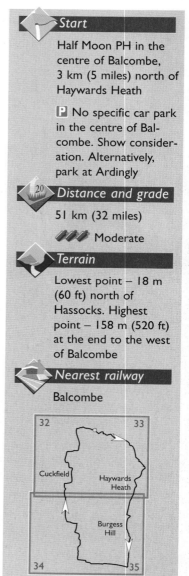

Start

Half Moon PH in the centre of Balcombe, 3 km (5 miles) north of Haywards Heath

P No specific car park in the centre of Balcombe. Show consideration. Alternatively, park at Ardingly

Distance and grade

51 km (32 miles)

Moderate

Terrain

Lowest point – 18 m (60 ft) north of Hassocks. Highest point – 158 m (520 ft) at the end to the west of Balcombe

Nearest railway

Balcombe

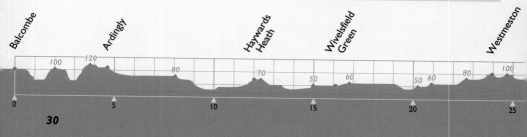

Wakehurst Place 4
Garden for all seasons with rare and exotic trees and shrubs. There are walks through a wooded valley, and around lakes and a bog garden

▲▼ *Wakehurst Place*

Half Moon PH, **Balcombe**
Gardeners Arms PH 🍺, Oak at Ardingly PH 🍺, Ardingly Inn PH, **Ardingly**
Cock PH 🍺, **Wivelsfield Green**
Victory Inn PH 🍺, Jolly Tanner PH 🍺, **Staplefield**

Bluebell Railway 4/5 *(off the route)*
Steam engines run on the 8 km (5 mile) line between Horsted Keynes, an old village with a spacious green that was once the centre of the medieval iron industry, and Sheffield Park with its period railway station. There is a collection of locomotives and rolling stock dating between 1865 and 1958

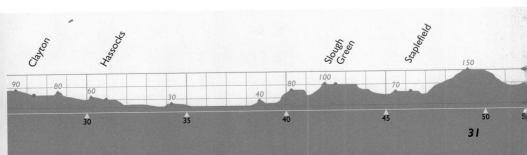

1 With back to the Half Moon PH bear L 'Ardingly, Haywards Heath, Lindfield'

2 1st L after Police Station onto Mill Lane 'Ardingly 2¾'

3 At T-j by letter box and triangle of grass R 'Ardingly'. Two steep climbs either side of reservoir

4 At T-j in Ardingly L then immediately R onto B2028 'Lindfield, Haywards Heath'

5 Busy section. Ignore 1st left to West Hoathly and the Bluebell Line. Take the next L onto Stone Cross Lane 'Horsted Keynes 2, Danehill 3½'

6 At T-j by triangle of grass at the end of Stone Cross Lane R 'Lindfield 1¾, Haywards Heath 3 ¾' then shortly 1st L onto Plummerden Lane 'Freshfield 1¾, Sheffield Park 4, North Common 5'

7 At T-j by triangle of grass R 'Walstead, Linfield, Haywards Heath'

8 After 2½ km (1½ miles) at the end of the cemetery to the right bear L (NS)

9 At T-j with B2111 L 'Scaynes Hill 1, Uckfield 11¼, Lewes 10¾'

10 Shortly, at T-j with A272 R 'Haywards Heath' then 1st L onto Slugwash Lane '7.5 ton weight limit'

➡ **two pages**

24 At X-roads with A272 at the end of Stairbridge Lane SA onto Buncton Lane

25 At T-j at the top of steady climb by triangle of grass R 'Cuckfield, Ansty'

26 At T-j with the B2115 at the end of Broxmead Lane L 'Warninglid 2' then after 800 m (½ mile) 1st R '6 ft 6 in width limit'

27 At X-roads at the end of Staplefield Lane R (NS)

28 At X-roads just past Victory Inn SA 'Brantridge Lane'

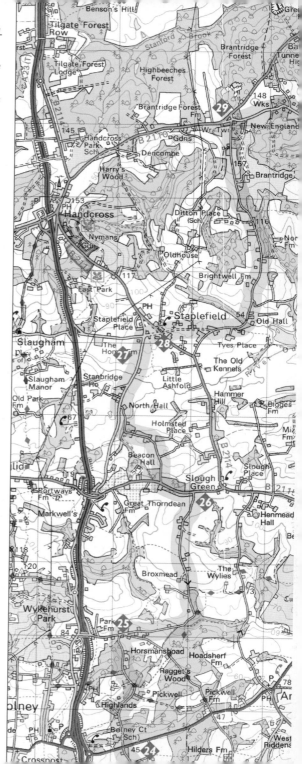

29 *Climb. Good views. After 4 km (2½ miles) at X-roads by red brick tower R onto Handcross Road 'Balcombe'*

30 *At T-j (with B2036) at the end of Handcross Road R 'Cuckfield, Burgess Hill' then 1st L onto Haywards Heath Road 'Haywards Heath, Lindfield, Ardingly' to return to start*

11 After 4 km (2½ miles) at T-j at the end of Slugwash Lane L then 1st R (NS). Shortly 1st R onto Hundred Acre Lane 'Streat 3, Westmeston 5'

12 At T-j L 'Streat 1½, Westmeston 3½' then R (same sign)

13 At T-j with B2116 at the end of Streat Lane R 'Westmeston ¾, Ditchling 2¼, Hassocks 4'

14 On sharp RH bend by church in Westmeston bear L (in effect SA) 'Underhill Lane, Narrow Road'

15 At X-roads SA (same sign)

16 At T-j with A273 at the end of Underhill Lane R then 1st L onto New Way Lane

17 At T-j with Randiddles Close L. At end of New Way Lane R onto Hassocks Road then 1st L onto College Lane 'Hurstpierpoint College'

18 Immediately after school L onto Chalkers Lane 'Hurstpierpoint'

19 After 800 m (½ mile) on sharp LH bend 1st R onto Danworth Lane

20 Cross stream, climb hill. At top 1st L onto Pomper Lane

21 At X-roads SA onto continuation of Pomper Lane

22 At T-j at the end of Pomper Lane L then after 800 m (½ mile) 1st R

23 At X-roads SA 'Stairbridge Lane'

24 At X-roads with A272 at the end of Stairbridge Lane SA onto Buncton Lane

◀ two pages

Between Ashdown Forest and the South Downs near Uckfield

6

Exposed sandstone flanks the roadside on the exit west from Uckfield, giving an indication of the underlying geology. The ride heads north, crossing several tributaries of the River Ouse that reaches the sea south of Newhaven. The first half of the route is a combination of fast descents down into the valleys, followed by short steep climbs out of them. Broadleaf woodlands alternate with prosperous arable farmland in this quintessential Sussex Weald countryside. The wooded areas are reminders of the great Forest of Anderida that once covered the slopes of the Weald. South of Hadlow Down, the route crosses into the area drained by the Cuckmere River. Two excellent pubs at Chiddingly and Ripe may tempt you to break the ride for some refreshments before turning north back to Uckfield.

Start

The Railway Station, Uckfield

P Long-term car parks off the top end of the High Street in Uckfield

Distance and grade

53 km (33 miles)

Moderate

Terrain

The northern section of the ride (the first half) is quite a roller coaster as no fewer than 8 streams are crossed, although all the climbs are short. The southern section is much flatter. Lowest point – 9 m (30 ft) between Ripe and Laughton. Highest point – 147 m (485 ft) at Hadlow Down

Nearest railway

Uckfield

Uckfield 1
Standing on a hillside above the valley of the River Ouse, Uckfield looks towards the great sweep of the downs. Traditional Sussex houses, brick and tile-hung, or weather boarded, line the attractive main street

Refreshments

Peacock PH 🍺, **Shortbridge**
Foresters Arms PH 🍺, **Fairwarp**
Maypole PH, **High Hurstwood**
Six Bells PH 🍺🍺, **Chiddingly**
Golden Cross PH, **Golden Cross**
Lamb Inn PH 🍺🍺, **Ripe**
Roebuck Inn PH, **Laughton**
Bluebell PH, **Shortgate**
Barley Mow PH, **Palehouse**

Fletching 2
Almost as old as the Ashdown Forest; one village inn dates from 1150

Ashdown Forest 5/8 (off the route)
Covers more than 5665 ha (14,000 acres) between the North and South Downs. Merely a remnant of the vast primeval Forest of Anderida that cut Sussex off from the rest of the country. It remained a wild and dangerous area until Elizabethan times when trees were felled to provide fuel for the forges of the Wealden iron industry

Charleston Farmhouse 20 (off the route)
The country home of artist Vanessa Bell, sister of writer Virginia Woolf and one of the Bloomsbury Group of writers and artists. Fireplaces, cupboards and every possible surface are decorated by the artist

Bentley Wildfowl Collection and Motor Museum 24 (off the route)
More than 100 species of geese, swans and ducks roam in the parkland. The motor museum has a changing collection of vintage and veteran cars, a formal garden, picnic spot and a woodland walk

Pooh Bridge,
own Forest

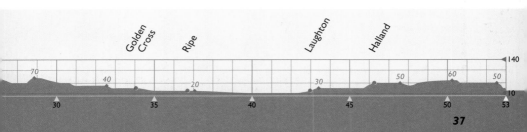

1 With back to the station R. At traffic lights SA up High Street. Climb hill past Post Office and turning on left to Civic Centre. At traffic lights with the Uckfield Cinque Ports Club to your right, turn L onto Church Street 'Buckswood Grange ½'

2 Follow signs for Haywards Heath and Piltdown. 400 m (¼ mile) after passing the Peacock Inn on your left next R 'Nutley'

3 At X-roads with A272 SA 'Down Street'

4 **Easy to miss.** After 3 km (2 miles) 1st R by triangle of grass 'Picketts Lane'

5 At T-j with A22 R 'Maresfield' then after 50 m (yd) 1st L (NS)

6 At T-j at the bottom of the hill, by triangle of grass R 'Fairwarp 1, Hartfield 7'

7 At T-j with the B2026 L then immediately R 'Fairwarp ½, Narrow Road'

8 Down then steeply uphill. At T-j with A26 at the top of Oldlands Hill R then L onto Perrymans Lane

9 At T-j at the end of Perrymans Lane L then 1st R 'Jarvis Brook 5, Rotherfield 6'

10 At X-roads at the end of Burnt Oak Road SA (NS)

11 At T-j at the bottom of short, steep hill R 'Hadlow Down 2, Buxted 4'

12 At X-roads with the A272 at the end of School Lane SA 'Blackboys 2¾, Framfield 4½'

13 At T-j at the bottom of long hill L 'Blackboys 1, Framfield 2¾' then L again immediately after bridge

14 At X-roads with B2102 SA 'Waldron 1¾, Horam 4'

15 At X-roads by small triangle of grass R onto Moat Lane

➡ *three pages*

28 Busy section. At roundabout bear R 'Town Centre ½' to return to start

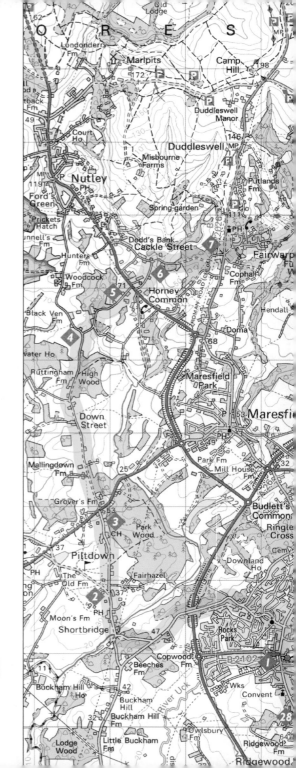

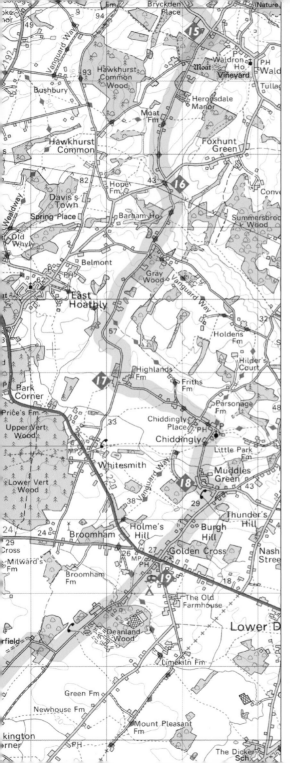

15 At X-roads by small triangle of grass R onto Moat Lane

16 Follow signs for Chiddingly. At offset X-roads R then L 'Chiddingly 2¾, Graywood 3¼'

17 Easy to miss. Keep following signs for Chiddingly. After 3 km (2 miles) opposite Coldharbour Farm on the right, turn L 'Chiddingly 1, Muddles Green 1¾'

18 Shortly after Chiddingly, at triangle of grass in Muddles Green, just past telephone box on right, turn R 'Golden Cross ¾, Lewes'

19 At X-roads with A22 SA onto path to the left of the Golden Cross PH to join the lane opposite

20 After 4 km (2½ miles) bear R by circle of grass in Ripe 'Laughton 2½, Firle 3¾, Lewes 7½' then shortly R again by triangle of grass 'Laughton 2½, East Hoathly 4¾'

21 At T-j at Mark Cross R 'Laughton 1¾, East Hoathly 4' then after 1 km (¾ mile) 1st L 'Laughton, Shortgate'

22 At X-roads with B2124 by Roebuck Inn SA 'Shortgate 1½, Halland 2½'

23 At T-j with B2192 R 'Halland 1¼, Heathfield 8, Hawkhurst 21'

24 Busy section. After 1 km (¾ mile) 1st L onto Knowle Lane 'Narrow Road'

25 At X-roads with A22 SA onto Sandhill Lane 'Narrow Road'

26 At X-roads L 'Palehouse ¾, Uckfield 2¾'

27 At T-j R 'Uckfield 1½'

◀ **three pages**

From Hailsham across the Pevensey Levels and over the Sussex Weald

7

Start

Leisure Centre, Hailsham

P As above

Distance and grade

53 km (33 miles)

Moderate/strenuous

This ride dispels the idea that southeast England consists of two ranges of hills, the North and South Downs, with a flat section between called the Weald. The ride starts very gently across the Pevensey Levels, but north of

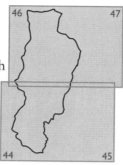

Terrain

From the flat Pevensey Levels to a very hilly middle section with four hills of over 91 m (300 ft) and more than 610 m (2000 ft) of climbing in total

Bodle Street Green, the going gets tougher. This is a ride of small lanes and woodland, an exploration of the countryside with no specific focal point. Beautiful wooded stretches alternate with open views, and if you have any energy left, you could always go for a swim at the leisure centre, where the ride starts and finishes.

Nearest railway

Polegate, 5 km (3 miles) south of Hailsham, or Stone gate Station, 2½ km (1½ miles) north of the top north east corner of the ride

Refreshments

Lots of choice in **Hailsham**
Welcome Stranger PH, **Windmill Hill**
White Horse PH 🍴, **Bodle Street Green**
Swan Inn 🍴🍴, **Wood's Corner**
Wheel PH 🍴, **Burwash Weald**
Kicking Donkey PH, **Witherenden Hill**
Star Inn 🍴🍴, **Old Heathfield**
Brewery Arms PH, **Vines Cross**

Michelham Priory, Upper Dicker *1-2*

West of Hailsham, slightly off the route, this priory was founded in 1229, but the moat and gatehouse were added in about 1400. After the Dissolution in 1536, the buildings were destroyed but were later repaired and incorporated into the Tudor house, which stands here today. The priory rooms contain exhibitions illustrating the way of life of the Augustinian monks. The rooms in the Tudor section contain some of the original furniture and original oak beams can be seen in the kitchen.

Pevensey Castle *4*

Built by the Romans as a coastal fort and added to by the Normans, these are very impressive ruins. The chapel, keep and dungeon remain and some sections were refortified for use in the Second World War.

Herstmonceux Castle *6*

Beautifully restored in the early 20th century, this medieval castle is in very good condition. Built around a courtyard, there are octagonal towers on each corner and three other semi-octagonal ones. The imposing entrance has a gatehouse with portcullis and battlements. It is not open to the public but can be viewed by following the footpath and bridleway southeast of Herstmonceux church.

Burwash *13*

Standing on a ridge between rivers, this village was once a centre for iron-making and the 14th-century iron tomb-slab inside the Church of St Bartholomew is indicative of this. Timbered shops and cottages give character to the long main street.

Bateman's, Burwash *13*

The home of Rudyard Kipling from 1902 to 1936, this 17th-century house originally belonged to an ironmaster. Kipling's study remains as it was and some of his books and poems and his Rolls Royce are on display. A restored watermill grinds corn in the garden.

Horam Manor *21*

This manor has been the home of famous vintage cider makers since 1947 and there are guided tours and audio-visual presentations.

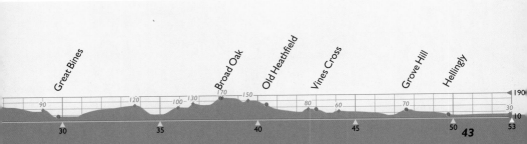

1 From the leisure centre L. At T-j with High Street R, then L onto George Street, staying in LH lane 'Eastbourne A295'

2 Opposite The Terminus PH L on Station Road 'Station Road Industrial Estate'

3 After 2½ km (1½ miles), on sharp RH bend by small circle of grass L (NS)

4 Easy to miss. After 3 km (2 miles), just before a long, low flint wall near a series of barns L 'Herstmonceux'

5 At T-j R 'Herstmonceux Castle and Church'. After 800 m (½ mile), opposite letter box 1st L 'Flowers Green' (Herstmonceux Castle is **not** open to the public)

6 At T-J in Flowers Green L (NS)

7 At T-j with A271 R 'Windmill Hill ½', then 1st L by petrol station on Victoria Road 'Bodle Street Green 1¾, Rushlake Green 5, Woods Corner 5'

8 After 3 km (2 miles) at White Horse PH in Bodle Street Green R 'Woods Corner 3½'

➡ **two pages**

22 After 6½ km (4 miles) at T-j with A271 R 'Eastbourne', then L on Hawks Road 'Hailsham 1'

23 At roundabout L 'Hailsham Industrial Estate'

24 In Hailsham, shortly after traffic lights by Battle Road at beginning of one-way system L onto Vicarage Lane 'Leisure Centre and Lagoon'

9 After 3 km (2 miles) at 1st triangle of grass bear R 'Woods Corner'. Shortly, at next T-j by triangle of grass L 'Woods Corner ¾'

10 At offset X-roads with B2096 by the Swan Inn SA 'Brightling 1¾'

11 After 1½ km (1 mile), just after Old Holbans Kennels 1st L 'Burwash 3, Batemans 4'

12 At X-roads after mast but before obelisk L on Willingford Lane 'Burwash Weald 2'

13 At T-j with A265 by The Wheel PH L (use pavement on far side if the road is very busy)

14 After 1 km (¾ mile) 1st R '7.5 ton wt limit'. At T-j R (NS)

15 After 3 km (2 miles) 1st L by Kicking Donkey PH

16 At T-j L 'Mayfield 4¼'

17 Ignore 1st left to Broad Oak by triangle of grass. After 5 km (3 miles) at T-j L 'Broad Oak'

18 After 4 km (2½ miles) at X-roads with A265 SA 'Heathfield Church 1½, Vines Cross 3¼' (or right for local shop)

19 At X-roads with B2096 SA through No Entry sign and **push** bike 50 m (yd)

20 At T-j L (NS). At next T-j by triangle of grass with a wooden bench beneath a chestnut tree R (NS)

↑ **Cuckoo Trail alternative**

The Cuckoo Trail is a converted railway path built by Sustrans running from Heathfield to Hailsham. To join it turn 1st R after the church in Old Heathfield. Bear L and once in Heathfield follow 'Cuckoo Trail' signs

21 Follow signs for Hailsham through Vines Cross. At T-j L 'Marle Green ½, Hellingly Hospital 3¾, Hailsham 5½'

◄ **two pages**

Through the eastern reaches of the Weald, north and east of Battle

To the east of the Ashdown Forest, the High Weald divides into three prongs, cut through deeply by the valleys of the Rivers Rother and Brede. Starting from Battle, the scene of the Battle of Hastings, this ride explores the middle of these three prongs, crossing the River Rother near Bodiam Castle and the River Brede near Whatlington. The first 5 km (3 miles) out of Battle are unavoidably on roads carrying more traffic than is ideal for cycle touring. However, once beyond Catsfield, you join a lane, sunk into a sandstone cutting, that gradually climbs up and down through rhododendrons north to Brightling, passing an eccentric tower near to instruction 6. Further north, the route crosses and recrosses the River Rother, passing the castle at Bodiam. Ewhurst Green has many delightful old buildings, including an odd wooden spire on the church.

Start

Tourist Information Centre, opposite the abbey, Battle

🅿 Mount Street, Battle (the road towards Whatlington, beyond the Kings Head PH)

Distance and grade

53 km (33 miles)

🚴🚴🚴 Moderate

Terrain

There are low points in the eastern half of the ride at the crossings of the Rivers Brede and Rother and their tributaries, all of which are followed by climbs, some are steep. The longest climb, of almost 91 m (300 ft), starts south of Brightling (instructions 8/9) Lowest point – 3 m (12 ft) at crossing of the River Rother near Bodiam. Highest point – 143 m (470 ft) at Brightling

Nearest railway

Battle

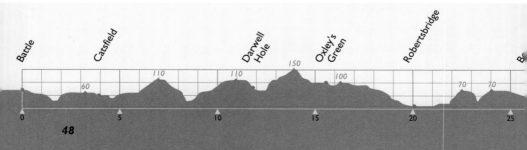

Battle 1

The Battle of Hastings was fought on the slopes below the town. On the site of his victory, William the Conqueror built an abbey. The high altar marks where Harold fell. Not much of the foundations and the monks' dormitory have survived

Penhurst 6 *(just off the route)*

Tiny hamlet with timeless church and manor farm. Ashburnham chapel has tombs of the family that owned nearby Ashburnham Place. Lumps of iron and stray cannonballs litter the countryside around Ashburnham Forge, one of the last foundries in Sussex, until its closure in the 1820s

▼ *Penshurst Village*

Brightling 9

Strange obelisks, domes, towers and a peculiar cone known as the Sugar Loaf are scattered around the village – follies of the 19th-century eccentric 'Mad Jack' Fuller, local squire and MP. He was buried under the 18 m (60 ft) high church-yard pyramid

Bodiam Castle 14/15

Picture-book castle with rounded corner towers, battlements and moat. Built in the 14th century it is remarkably intact. There are airy views from the roof across the surrounding parkland scattered with oaks. Restored traction engines are on display at the Quarry Farm Steam Museum

Refreshments

Plenty of choice in **Battle**
Jack Fuller PH 🍽, **Oxley's Green**
Seven Stars PH, **Robertsbridge**
Salehurst Halt PH 🍽, **Salehurst**
Curlew Inn, Castle Inn, **Bodiam**
White Dog Inn 🍽, **Ewhurst Green**
Rose & Crown PH, **Beckley**

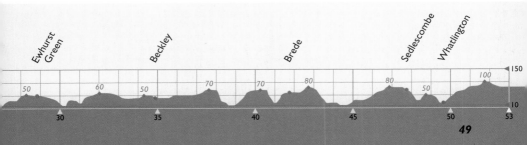

1 With back to the Tourist Information Centre L out of Battle on the A2100 towards Hastings. After 600 m (yd) 1st R at the edge of town onto Powdermill Lane 'B2095 Catsfield 2½'

2 At T-j with B2204 (formerly A269) L 'Bexhill 6, Catsfield ½'

3 Very busy section. Shortly after White Hart PH R onto Skinners Lane (NS)

4 After 2 km (1¼ miles) 1st R by triangle of grass by Birch Cottage (NS)

5 At T-j with B2204 R 'Penshurst 2, Battle 3½' then shortly 1st L before telephone box '6 ft 6 in width limit'

6 Steep descent, passing unusual tower. At top of hill 1st R 'Brightling'

7 At T-j R 'Brightling 2½'

8 At X-roads with B2096 SA 'Brightling 1'

9 Ignore 1st right to Mountfield / Robertsbridge. Towards the top of the hill with church 200 m (yd) ahead R by triangle of grass 'Robertsbridge 4'

10 After 6½ km (4 miles) at T-j in Robertsbridge L 'Salehurst, Hurst Green'

➡ **two pages**

26 At T-j with B2244 at the end of Hurst Lane L 'Hastings 7' then 1st R 'Spilsted Vineyard'. At T-j bear R

27 At X-roads with A21 SA 'Leeford Vineyards ½' then at T-j by triangle of grass L downhill '7.5 ton weight limit'

28 Last climb. At T-j at the end of Mount Street L to return to the start

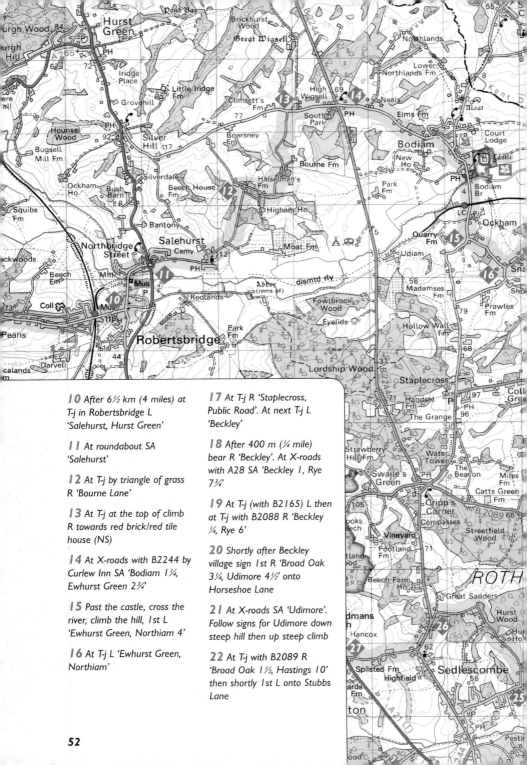

10 After 6½ km (4 miles) at T-j in Robertsbridge L 'Salehurst, Hurst Green'

11 At roundabout SA 'Salehurst'

12 At T-j by triangle of grass R 'Bourne Lane'

13 At T-j at the top of climb R towards red brick/red tile house (NS)

14 At X-roads with B2244 by Curlew Inn SA 'Bodiam 1¼, Ewhurst Green 2¾'

15 Past the castle, cross the river, climb the hill, 1st L 'Ewhurst Green, Northiam 4'

16 At T-j L 'Ewhurst Green, Northiam'

17 At T-j R 'Staplecross, Public Road'. At next T-j L 'Beckley'

18 After 400 m (¼ mile) bear R 'Beckley'. At X-roads with A28 SA 'Beckley 1, Rye 7¾'

19 At T-j (with B2165) L then at T-j with B2088 R 'Beckley ¼, Rye 6'

20 Shortly after Beckley village sign 1st R 'Broad Oak 3¼, Udimore 4½' onto Horseshoe Lane

21 At X-roads SA 'Udimore'. Follow signs for Udimore down steep hill then up steep climb

22 At T-j with B2089 R 'Broad Oak 1½, Hastings 10' then shortly 1st L onto Stubbs Lane

23 Down then up. At fork near the top bear R then at T-j with A28 at the end of Stubb Lane turn R

24 Busy section. Use pavement with discretion. 1st L onto Pottery Lane 'Sedlescombe 3, Battle 6¼'

25 Easy to miss. Ignore two right turns with width limit

signs (the second is signposted 'Broad Oak'). Take the next R almost opposite Brede Barn Farm onto Hurst Lane

26 At T-j with B2244 at the end of Hurst Lane L 'Hastings 7' then 1st R 'Spilsted Vineyard'. At T-j bear R

three pages

South from Tenterden to Rye

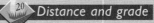
Start

Tourist Information Centre, Tenterden

P Follow signs

Distance and grade

53 km (33 miles)

Easy

Terrain

From the very flat to the gently undulating. Two hills of 61 m (200 ft), west of Rye then north of Udimore

Nearest railway

Appledore or Rye

An easy ride through the flat moors and marshes of west Kent and East Sussex. The lane across Shirley Moor is a real delight, with a refreshment stop at Appledore to look forward to. A straight section alongside the Military Canal leads to the charms of Rye, one of the Cinque Ports. Two gentle climbs west, then north through woodlands drop you back on the levels at the bridge over the Otter Channel.

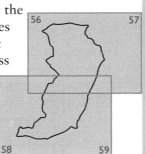

56   57

58   59

Refreshments

Lots of choice in **Tenterden**
Red Lion PH, Swan PH, Sentry Box Tea Rooms, **Appledore**
Mermaid PH 🍴🍴, lots of choice in **Rye**
Bull Inn, Kings Head PH **Udimore**
Coffee and tea at Flackley Ash Hotel, **Peasmarsh**
Ewe and Lambs PH, **Wittersham**
Wine and ale bar, wine tasting, tea and coffee at **Tenterden Vineyards, Small Hythe**

Tenterden   Brook Street   Appledore Heath   Appledore   Stone Bridge   Scot's Float   Rye

60

20

0   5   10   15   20   25

Appledore 5

Originally on the coast, Appledore was an important ship-building centre. During the Napoleonic Wars, the Royal Military Canal was constructed and a short section of it is now preserved by the National Trust. In the village are many interesting buildings from various periods.

Rye 6-7

This beautiful hilltop town has had a turbulent history: it was partially destroyed by the sea in the 14th-century, frequently attacked by the French and nearly burned

▲ Rye

down in 1377. It enjoyed privileged status as a Cinque Port town and was an important trading point with merchants, pirates and smugglers. Although the sea has retreated, the town is still surrounded by three rivers and has well-preserved 16th-century timbered houses, 18th-century winding cobbled streets and many places of interest including:

The Landgate

Built by Edward III in 1329, this gateway was the only means of entering the town at high tide.

Mermaid Inn

This inn was founded in the 11th-century and became the headquarters of an infamous smuggling gang. Mermaid Street is one of the prettiest in Rye.

Ypres Tower

This tower is one of the oldest surviving buildings in Rye; it was built in 1250 to protect the town from the French.

Small Hythe 14-1

Smallhythe Place is an early 16th-century house that was originally a port house and shipyard; it later belonged to the actress Dame Ellen Terry and now contains displays of theatrical memorabilia. Nearby are the Tenterden Vineyards where the winery and processing equipment can be seen and then the wine tasted; there is also a large herb garden.

The Hermitage   Peasmarsh   Wittersham   Peening Quarter   Small Hythe

60   20   40   50 60   40   20   30   20   40   60   60
                                                                                              10
30   35   40   45   50   53

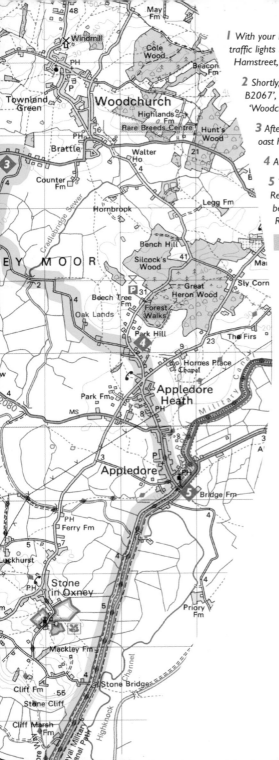

1 With your back to the Tourist Information Centre L. At traffic lights SA, then 1st R on Oaks Road 'New Romney, Hamstreet, Woodchurch, Appledore'

2 Shortly, on RH bend L 'Woodchurch, Hamstreet B2067', then at X-roads SA onto Woodchurch Road 'Woodchurch 4½, Hamstreet 7½, Hythe B2067'

3 After 5 km (3 miles), shortly after passing the oast house of Ditton Farm on your left turn R (NS)

4 At T-j at the end of Moor Lane R (NS)

5 Through Appledore. Shortly after passing Red Lion and Swan PHs, at traffic lights just before bridge over canal turn R 'Iden Lock 3, Rye 6'

➡ *next page*

14 At T-j with B2082 by Ewe and Lambs PH L 'Tenterden, Rolvenden'. Follow the B2082 for 7 km (4½ miles) back to Tenterden

6 After 10 km (6 miles), at T-j with A268 L 'Camber, Hastings, Battle'. Follow signs for Town Centre

7 (Visit Rye) At roundabout past Tourist Information Centre R 'Battle 14 (B2089)'

8 8 km (5 miles) after leaving Rye and 1½ km (1 mile) after passing the Kings Head PH in Udimore (the pub is some way after the first 'Udimore' sign), 1st R 'Beckley, Peasmarsh'

9 After 1½ km (1 mile) 1st R 'Hayes Lane, Narrow road'

10 At T-j by triangle of grass R 'Peasmarsh'

11 At T-j by Peasmarsh Place L

12 **Easy to miss.** After 800 m (½ mile) 1st L shortly after white boarded house and red-brick bungalow

13 At X-roads with A268 SA 'Wittersham'

◄ **previous page**

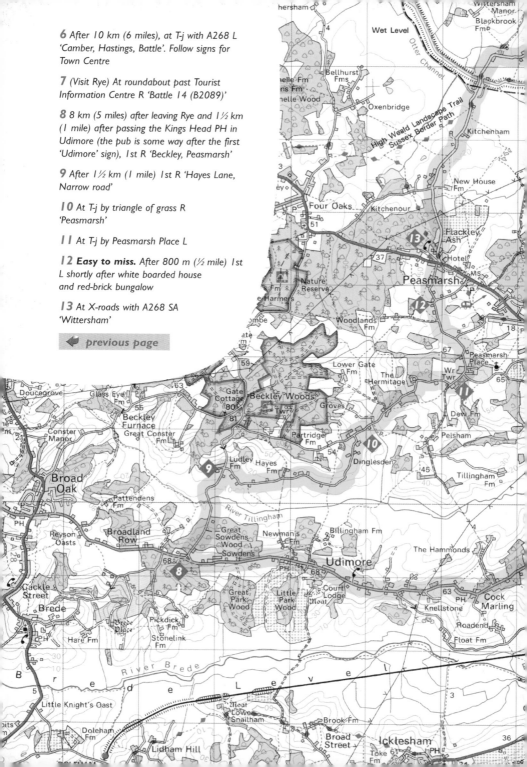

10 *Tenterden to Sissinghurst Castle*

A satisfying ride that takes in points of interest such as Sissinghurst Castle and the windmill at Woodchurch, the attractive villages of Headcorn, Smarden and Pluckley, some good pubs and wonderful scenery.

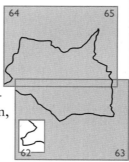

Although the road between Tenterden and Sissinghurst is at times busy, this is soon forgotten as you turn off towards the old-world beauty of Sissinghurst Castle. The bridlepath that takes you through the estate may at times be a little rough but this diversion from the main road and past such a magnificent property is fine compensation for any slight discomfort.

Start

Tourist Information Centre, Tenterden

P Follow signs

Distance and grade

53 km (33 miles)

Easy/moderate

Terrain

Fairly flat or gentle, undulating hills. One climb worth noting: 82 m (270 ft) between Smarden and Pluckley

Nearest railway

Pluckley

Refreshments

Lots of choice in **Tenterden**
Bull Inn 🍴, **Sissinghurst**
Coffee and tea at **Sissinghurst Castle**
Bell and Jorrods PH, **Frittenden**
Kings Arms PH, George and Dragon PH 🍴, **Headcorn**
The Bell PH 🍴🍴, Smarden Bell PH, Chequers PH 🍴, **Smarden**
Black Horse PH 🍴, **Pluckley**
Dering Arms PH 🍴🍴, **Pluckley Station**
Bonny Cravat PH, Six Bells PH, **Woodchurch**

Tenterden — Parkgate — Fosters Green — Golford — Sissinghurst — Sissinghurst Castle — Frittenden — Headcorn

50 60 70 60 60 70 50 50

0   5   10   15   20   25

Sissinghurst Garden 3

These gardens were created by Vita Sackville West and her husband Sir Harold Nicholson in the 1930s. A series of small gardens are enclosed within the remains of an Elizabethan mansion.

Headcorn Flower Centre and Vineyard 7-8

Award-winning wine is produced at this vineyard and can be tasted free of charge at the end of a visit. Chrysanthemums and orchid lilies bloom all year round in the flower houses and there is a large reservoir stocked with trout.

Smarden 10

This an old wool village with an Elizabethan market place and many interesting old buildings. The large parish church has a copy of an Elizabethan charter granting permission for a weekly market and an annual fair.

Woodchurch Windmill 14-15

This restored smock mill, now in working order, contains an exhibition charting the mill's history.

Rare Breeds Centre, Woodchurch 15

Ninety acres of farmland house this important collection of rare animals. There is a 'kiddies corner' where many young animals can be handled.

Tenterden 16-17

The name Tenterden comes from the earliest settlement: a pig pasture for the men of Thanet. By the 14th-century, sheep were the main source of wealth and a flourishing cloth industry developed. Tenterden prospered and became a member of the Confederation of the Cinque Ports. St Mildred's Church dominates the main street with its impressive pinnacled tower built in the 15th-century of Bethersden marble. The 13th-century chancel is the oldest section of the church and has an early English lancet window with a modern stained glass representation of St Mildred. The Woolpack Inn and the Tudor Rose date from the 15th century and, unlike some other buildings in the High Street (such as the Eight Bells Inn), have not been given 18th- or 19th-century facades.

The Tenterden and District Museum 17

This explains the town's interesting history and also houses a railway museum. The main station nearby was closed in 1954 but now runs steam train trips into the Wealden countryside.

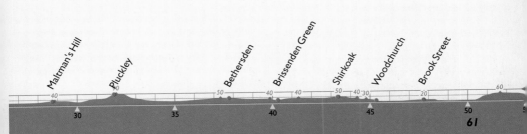

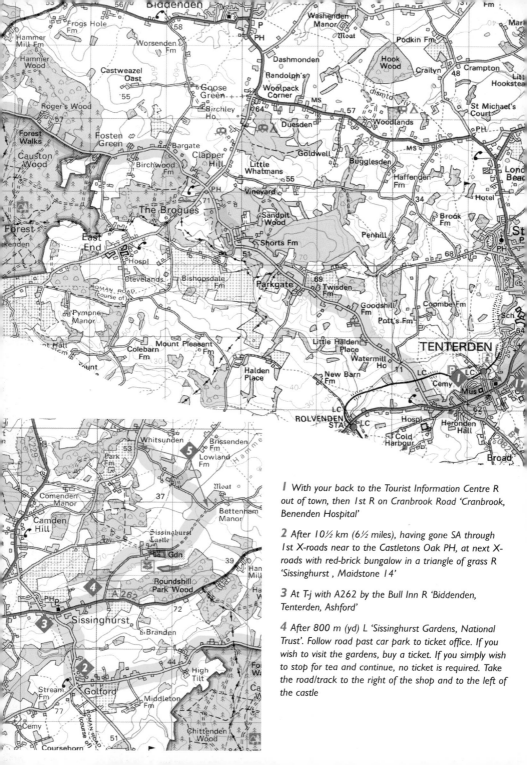

1 With your back to the Tourist Information Centre R out of town, then 1st R on Cranbrook Road 'Cranbrook, Benenden Hospital'

2 After 10½ km (6½ miles), having gone SA through 1st X-roads near to the Castletons Oak PH, at next X-roads with red-brick bungalow in a triangle of grass R 'Sissinghurst , Maidstone 14'

3 At T-j with A262 by the Bull Inn R 'Biddenden, Tenterden, Ashford'

4 After 800 m (yd) L 'Sissinghurst Gardens, National Trust'. Follow road past car park to ticket office. If you wish to visit the gardens, buy a ticket. If you simply wish to stop for tea and continue, no ticket is required. Take the road/track to the right of the shop and to the left of the castle

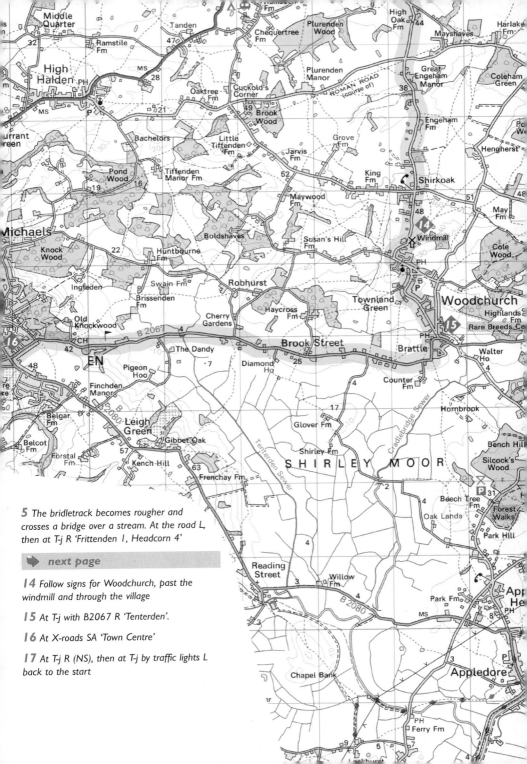

5 The bridletrack becomes rougher and crosses a bridge over a stream. At the road L, then at T-j R 'Frittenden 1, Headcorn 4'

➡ **next page**

14 Follow signs for Woodchurch, past the windmill and through the village

15 At T-j with B2067 R 'Tenterden'.

16 At X-roads SA 'Town Centre'

17 At T-j R (NS), then at T-j by traffic lights L back to the start

6 Through Frittenden, following signs for Headcorn. At T-j R 'Headcorn ¼, Lenham 7'

7 At X-roads with A274 R on North Street 'Biddenden, Tenterden'

8 On sharp RH bend at end of village L 'Smarden'

9 At T-j by The Bell PH L 'Smarden', then 1st R 'Smarden'

10 In Smarden at T-j by Chequers PH L

11 After 5½ km (3½ miles), in Pluckley at top of the hill R 'Bethersden'

12 After 5½ km (3½ miles) you will pass a timber frame works. At X-roads SA 'Great Chart, Ashford', then 1st R on Kiln Lane

13 At T-j with A28 L (NS), then after 800 m (½ mile) 1st R ' Woodchurch 4'

← *previous page*

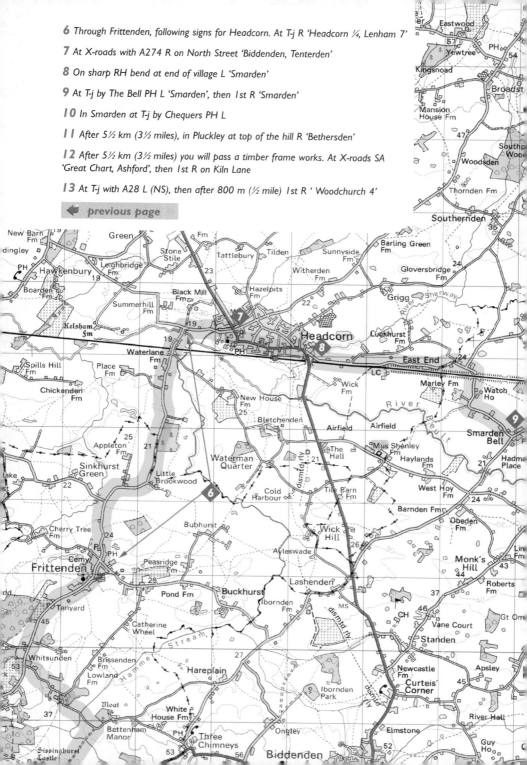

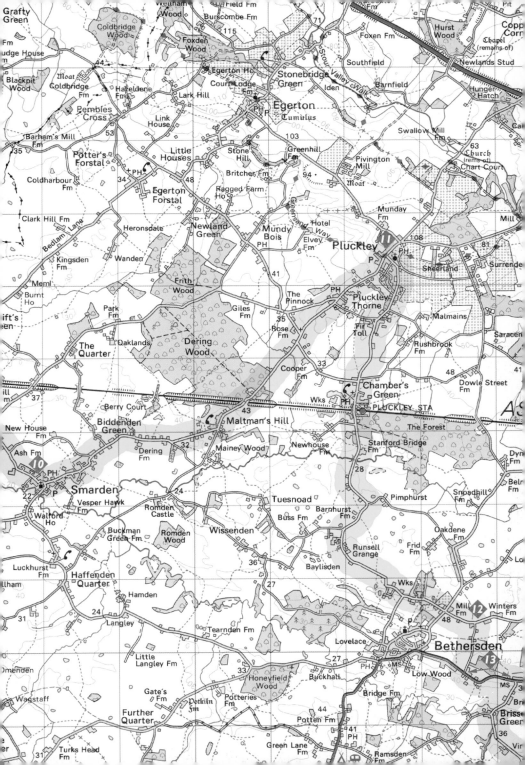

Wye to Chilham

This his ride features lots of stretches of beautiful lanes linked together in an exploration of the rolling downland between the A20/M20 and the A2/M2. The scenery is typical of Kent, with many oast houses, orchards and fields of hops. The village of Chilham is a real delight with pubs, tea shops and a castle to visit. The ride finishes with some lovely wooded lanes through Sole Street and Crundale.

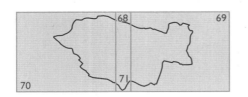

Start

The church in Wye

P Follow signs to free parking near start

Distance and grade

51 km (32 miles)
Moderate

Terrain

Two climbs of 122 m (400 ft) – between Westwell and Charing Hill and between Shalmsford Street and Sole Street. Several short, steep hills, The Wynd just north of Charing is fiercesome!

Nearest railway

Wye

Refreshments

New Flying Horse PH 🍺, Tickled Trout PH 🍺, **Wye**
Flying Horse PH 🍺🍺, **Boughton Lees**
Wheel Inn, **Westwell**
Bowl Inn, **north of Charing Hill**
The Plough PH 🍺, **Shottenden**
White Horse PH 🍺🍺, Woolpack PH 🍺,
tea shops, **Chilham**
Ye Olde England PH, **Shalmsford Street**
Compasses PH 🍺, **Sole Street**

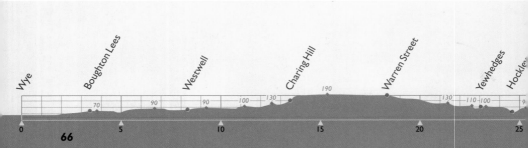

Wye 1

There are good views across the Stour Valley from this unspoilt market town. The Church of St Gregory and St Martin houses some interesting collections. Also interesting is Wye College, founded in the 15th-century by John Kempe (who later became Archbishop of Canterbury) and now an agricultural college.

▲ Chilham Castle

Agricultural Museum, Brook 1

Slightly off the route, a wide collection of farm implements is displayed in a 14th-century tithe barn and a 19th-century oast house.

Doddington Place Gardens 4

Beautiful rhododendrons and azaleas, a sunken garden, a rock garden and expansive lawns can be found within these 10 acres of landscaped garden.

Chilham 20-21

The village grew up around the gates of the medieval castle. The central square is dominated by St Mary's Church and narrow streets full of pretty cottages lead off from this.

Chilham Castle 20

Only the octagonal keep remains of the original Norman castle; the present castle was completed in 1616 and stands between the medieval ruins and the village and is not open to the public. The large gardens contain a lake, a rose garden, a deer park and a 'petland' for children.

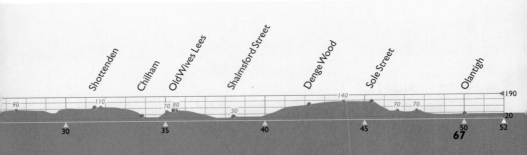

Shottenden · Chilham · Old Wives Lees · Shalmsford Street · Denge Wood · Sole Street · Olantigh

1 With your back to the church go SA down the main street past the shops. At T-j by Methodist chapel R

2 Over the bridge and 1st L 'Ashford 4, Faversham 12'

3 At X-roads with A28 SA 'Boughton Lees'

4 In Boughton Lees, before Flying Horse PH by village green L, then at T-j with A251 L 'Kennington, Ashford'

5 After 1½ km (1 mile) 1st R 'Potters Corner, Westwell', then immediately R again on Lenacre Street 'Westwell'

➧ *next page*

16 At T-j with A251 L (NS), then R 'Badlesmere Church, Fisher St, Molash'

17 At T-j R 'Fisher St, Shottenden, Chilham'

18 Follow signs for Shottenden. At T-j R 'Shottenden ½, Chilham 2'

19 At next T-j L 'Chilham 1¾, Canterbury 8'

20 At T-j with A252 L 'Ashford, Canterbury', then R 'Chilham'

21 (Explore Chilham) From the square, facing the White Horse PH turn L downhill to X-roads with A252. SA '6 ft 6 ins width limit'

22 At next X-roads SA 'Old Wives Lees'

23 At T-j R then L onto Lower Lees Road (Pilgrims Way) 'Chartham 3, Canterbury 6'

24 At T-j with A28 L 'Canterbury, Shalmsford Street ½, Chart 1½', then R 'Shalmsford Street

25 Shortly after crossing bridge over railway next R onto Bobbin Lodge Hill

26 At T-j L then after 600 m (yd) R 'Sole Street, Waltham' on Penny Pot Lane

27 After 5½ km (3½ miles) at X-roads R 'Sole Street, Crundale'.

28 At T-j R 'Godmersham 1¾, Canterbury 9'

29 At next T-j L 'Wye 2¼, Brook 2' to return to Wye

4 In Boughton Lees, before Flying Horse PH by village green L, then at T-j with A251 L 'Kennington, Ashford'

5 After 1½ km (1 mile) 1st R 'Potters Corner, Westwell', then immediately R again on Lenacre Street 'Westwell'

6 In Westwell at offset X-roads SA 'Charing 3¾, Maidstone 16¼'

7 After 1½ km (1 mile) 2nd R on LH bend just after large red-brick house 'Charing'

8 At T-j after 2½ km (1½ miles) R (NS)

9 At T-j with A252 at the end of Pett Lane R, then 1st L on The Wynd (very steep), then at T-j L

10 At X-roads near Bowl Inn PH SA 'Warren Street 2, Lenham 4'

11 At T-j at end of Wareditch Road R 'Stalisfield 2¾'

12 After 5 km (3 miles), shortly after passing, on your left, a turning to Newnham and Doddington by a large oak tree and then Wingfield Farm take next R (NS)

13 At T-j R 'Throwley, Sheldwich'

14 At T-j L 'Throwley 1¼, Sheldwich 3, Faversham 5', then 1st R 'Belmont ¾, Throwley 1, Sheldwich 2'

15 After 1 km (¾ mile), on sharp RH bend L 'Badlesmere, Sheldwich'

16 At T-j with A251 L (NS), then R 'Badlesmere Church, Fisher St, Molash'

17 At T-j R 'Fisher St, Shottenden, Chilham'

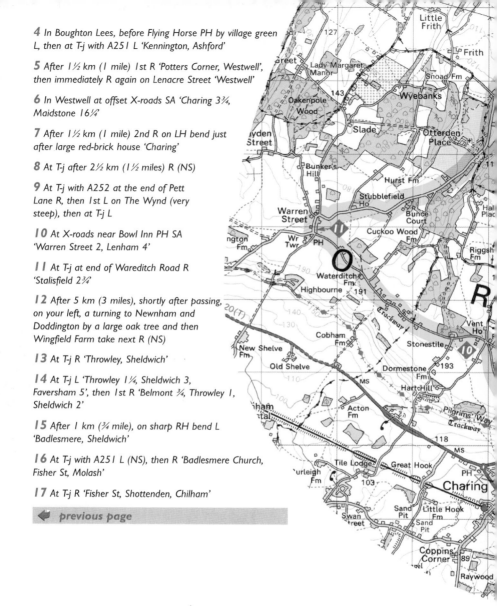

◀ **previous page**

Narrow lanes and extensive views on the eastern end of the North Downs

This is a Chinese puzzle of a ride with as many instructions as there are miles covered. It links together short sections of beautiful, wooded, steep twisting lanes at the eastern end of the North Downs. The whole area is a maze of little lanes, ideal for exploration by bike if you are not in a pressing hurry to get from A to B. There are many points along the ride with good views, but the best are from Farthing Common with the downs spreading away to the northwest and the English Channel to the south.

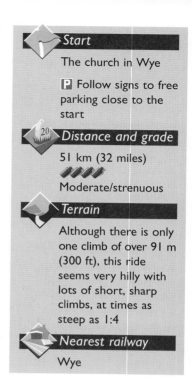

Start

The church in Wye

P Follow signs to free parking close to the start

Distance and grade

51 km (32 miles)

Moderate/strenuous

Terrain

Although there is only one climb of over 91 m (300 ft), this ride seems very hilly with lots of short, sharp climbs, at times as steep as 1:4

Nearest railway

Wye

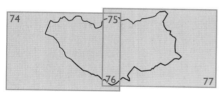

Refreshments

Tickled Trout PH 🍺, New Flying Horse PH 🍺, tea shops, **Wye**
Compasses PH 🍺, **Sole Street**
Lord Nelson PH, **Waltham**
Star Inn, **Bossingham**
Duke of Cumberland PH 🍺, **Barham**
Jackdaw PH, **Denton**
Endeavour PH, **Wootton**
Coach and Horses PH, **Lyminge**
Tiger Inn 🍺🍺, **Stowting**

Places of interest

Parsonage Farm Rural Heritage Centre 23
The history of domestic animals is displayed at this farm and there are many rare and traditional breeds to be seen. A small exhibition tells the story of the farm.

Lyminge 24
Most of Lyminge is Victorian but its history begins in 633 when King Ethelbert's daughter and Bishop Paulinus founded an abbey here. Some of the original walls were incorporated into the village church.

Saltwood Castle 26
Slightly off the route, this castle was probably built by a Warden of the Cinque Ports in 1160. It is said that the four knights who murdered Thomas Becket in 1170 stayed overnight here on their way to Canterbury. By the 14th century, the inner bailey walls and towers were completed and in the 1380s the Archbishop William Courtenay added the triangular outer bailey, the gatehouse to the inner bailey, inscribed with his arms, and some domestic buildings. Much was damaged in an earthquake in 1580 but some parts have been well restored.

Wye Downs 31
These form part of the North Downs and are covered with woodland and shrubs. The area is a nature reserve.

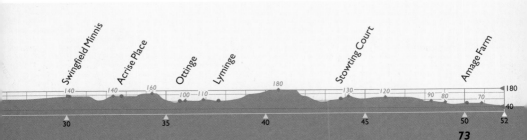

1 With your back to the church, facing the main street L out of town, then 1st L on Olantigh Road by telephone box 'Crundale'

2 Shortly after passing stately manor house on left (Olantigh), at top of small hill turn R 'Olantigh Nurseries'

3 After 400 m (yd) at triangle of grass L (sign broken)

4 In Crundale at bottom of hill on sharp LH bend R (in effect SA) 'Crundale Church 1½'

5 Steep hill. At T-j R (NS). At X-roads R 'Waltham, Hastingleigh'

6 At T-j at end of Richdore Road, by a triangle of grass L 'Petham 2¼, Canterbury 7', then 1st R by Lord Nelson PH onto Church Lane

7 At T-j R 'Elmsted 2, Hastingleigh 3, Ashford 10', then 1st L

8 At T-j with B2068 L (NS), then 1st R. At T-j R (NS)

➡ **three pages**

27 Views of the sea to the left. At T-j with B2068 R, then 1st L 'Monks Horton, Stowting'

28 At X-roads R 'Stowting, Brabourne'

29 After 2½ km (1½ miles), at 4-way junction just before sign for Brabourne bear R (in effect SA) 'Brook, Wye'

30 After 2 km (1¼ miles), shortly after left turning to Brabourne, as road climbs escarpment L downhill 'Brook 3, Wye 2½'

31 At T-j by triangle of grass R 'Wye 1¾, Canterbury 13'

32 At T-j L 'Wye ½'

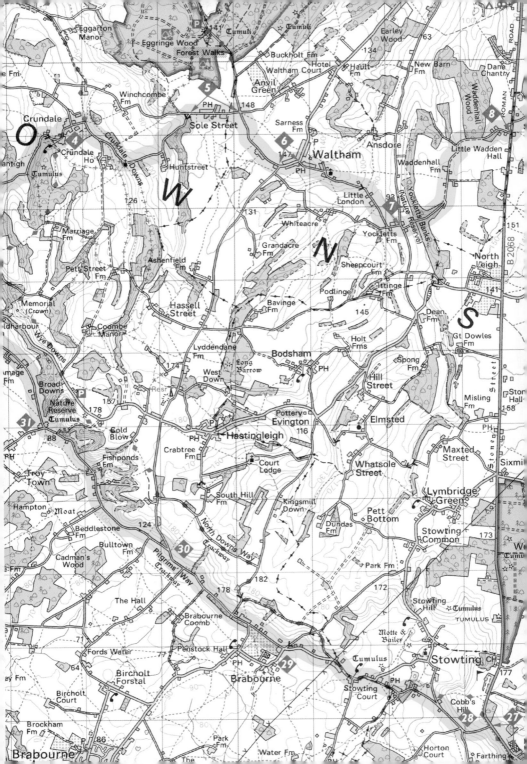

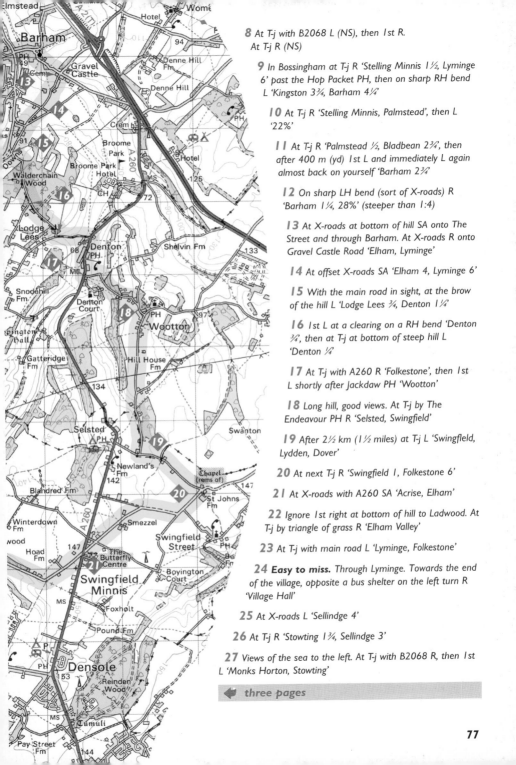

8 At T-j with B2068 L (NS), then 1st R. At T-j R (NS)

9 In Bossingham at T-j R 'Stelling Minnis 1½, Lyminge 6' past the Hop Packet PH, then on sharp RH bend L 'Kingston 3¾, Barham 4¼'

10 At T-j R 'Stelling Minnis, Palmstead', then L '22%'

11 At T-j R 'Palmstead ½, Bladbean 2¾', then after 400 m (yd) 1st L and immediately L again almost back on yourself 'Barham 2¾'

12 On sharp LH bend (sort of X-roads) R 'Barham 1¼, 28%' (steeper than 1:4)

13 At X-roads at bottom of hill SA onto The Street and through Barham. At X-roads R onto Gravel Castle Road 'Elham, Lyminge'

14 At offset X-roads SA 'Elham 4, Lyminge 6'

15 With the main road in sight, at the brow of the hill L 'Lodge Lees ¾, Denton 1¼'

16 1st L at a clearing on a RH bend 'Denton ¾', then at T-j at bottom of steep hill L 'Denton ¼'

17 At T-j with A260 R 'Folkestone', then 1st L shortly after Jackdaw PH 'Wootton'

18 Long hill, good views. At T-j by The Endeavour PH R 'Selsted, Swingfield'

19 After 2½ km (1½ miles) at T-j L 'Swingfield, Lydden, Dover'

20 At next T-j R 'Swingfield 1, Folkestone 6'

21 At X-roads with A260 SA 'Acrise, Elham'

22 Ignore 1st right at bottom of hill to Ladwood. At T-j by triangle of grass R 'Elham Valley'

23 At T-j with main road L 'Lyminge, Folkestone'

24 **Easy to miss.** Through Lyminge. Towards the end of the village, opposite a bus shelter on the left turn R 'Village Hall'

25 At X-roads L 'Sellindge 4'

26 At T-j R 'Stowting 1¾, Sellindge 3'

27 Views of the sea to the left. At T-j with B2068 R, then 1st L 'Monks Horton, Stowting'

◀ **three pages**

Sandwich and quiet Kent villages in the southeastern corner of England

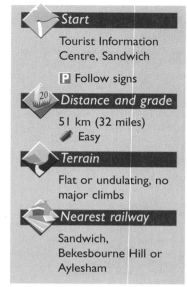

Start

Tourist Information Centre, Sandwich

P Follow signs

Distance and grade

51 km (32 miles)
Easy

Terrain

Flat or undulating, no major climbs

Nearest railway

Sandwich, Bekesbourne Hill or Aylesham

Starting at Sandwich, one of the Cinque Ports and a very attractive old town, the ride takes in the gentle, rolling countryside of the eastern part of Kent. As the ride moves west, you start passing the orchards of fruit trees that give Kent its sobriquet 'The garden of England'.

Next come the picturesque villages of Littlebourne and Wickhambreaux. The final stretch through Preston and Goldstone gives one the impression of being at the extremity of a country, even though the Isle of Thanet and Margate lie further east and north. Just before your return to Sandwich, you pass the ruins of Richborough Castle.

80	81
82	83

Refreshments

Lots of choice in **Sandwich**
Hare and Hounds PH, **Northbourne**
Butchers Arms PH, **Studdal** Crown Inn, **Eythorne**
White Horse PH, **Lower Eythorne**
Yew Tree PH, **Barfrestone**
Bulls Head PH, **Adisham**
King William IV PH, The Anchor PH, **Littlebourne**
Rose Inn 🍷, **Wickhambreaux**
Half Moon PH, **Preston**

Sandwich — Ham — Northbourne — Sutton — East Studdal — Ashley — Eythorne — Lower Eythorne — Barfrestone — Frogham — Ratling — Ad...

0 — 5 — 10 — 15 — 20 — 25

Sandwich *1*
Sandwich is an excellently preserved medieval town with many interesting buildings. It was one of the original Cinque Ports when the Confederation was formed by Edward the Confessor in 1050. In return for many privileges, these towns provided ships and the men to work on them.

Guildhall *1*
Built during the reign of Elizabeth I, the Guildhall has since been modified but still has many interesting historical and architectural features. An oak screen dating from 1300 is on display in the Courtroom.

The Butts *1*
The original town wall was built in 1384 and part of it remains.

Strand Street *1*
Many of the town's oldest buildings are on this street: St Mary's Church was built on the site of a Saxon Nunnery by the Normans; the 'Sandwich Weavers' was used as a workshop and home by 16th-century Dutch refugees; 'The Pilgrims' are 14th-century merchant houses with overhanging upper floors.

Northbourne Court *5-6*
This garden has Saxon origins but its terraced structure is Jacobean. It consists of several small gardens enclosed by high walls and there is great character shown in the unusual selection of plants.

Goodnestone Park Gardens, near Wingham *15*
A large garden, surrounded by parkland, with formal terraces and some unusual plants and trees. Jane Austen visited many times.

Howletts Zoo Park, Bekesbourne *17-18*
Specialising in breeding rare animals, this zoo has elephants, tigers, cheetah, deer and one of the largest gorilla colonies in the world.

Richborough Castle *22-23*
The Romans landed here in AD 43 and called their settlement 'Rutupiae'; a monument was erected in AD 85 but only rubble survives. In the 3rd century, it was fortified with a triple line of ditches but was soon replaced by a Saxon Shore Fort, one of a series built to protect the coast. Three massive sets of walls remain. A little way south is the 'Gallows Field', the town's execution site.

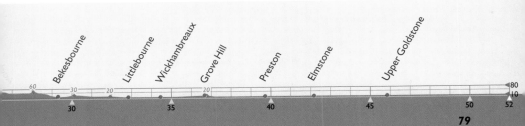

1 From the Tourist Information Centre L, then sharp R onto Delf Street past Fleur de Lys PH. SA on King Street. At T-j by Millwall Place R, then L 'Station'

2 After 1½ km (1 mile) at roundabout L, 'A258 Deal', then 2nd R on Mill Lane 'Ham'

3 After 1 km (¾ mile) 1st L by triangle of grass 'Finglesham, Deal'

➡ **two pages**

18 At X-roads with A257 in Littlebourne SA onto Margate Street 'Ickham, Wickhambreaux'

19 Follow signs for Preston through Wickhambreaux. After 5 km (3 miles) by triangle of grass R 'Preston 1¼, Wingham 3¾'

20 At T-j with B2046 in Preston R 'Wingham, Canterbury', then L opposite village stores and phone box 'Elmstone ¾, Westmarsh 3'

21 Follow signs for Elmstone then Westmarsh. On RH bend after 1½ km (1 mile) L towards church 'Sheerwater ¾, Hoaden 1¼, Westmarsh 1½'

22 Follow signs for Ware then Richborough. At T-j / X-roads L 'Richborough'

23 At T-j by fire station in Sandwich L to return to town centre

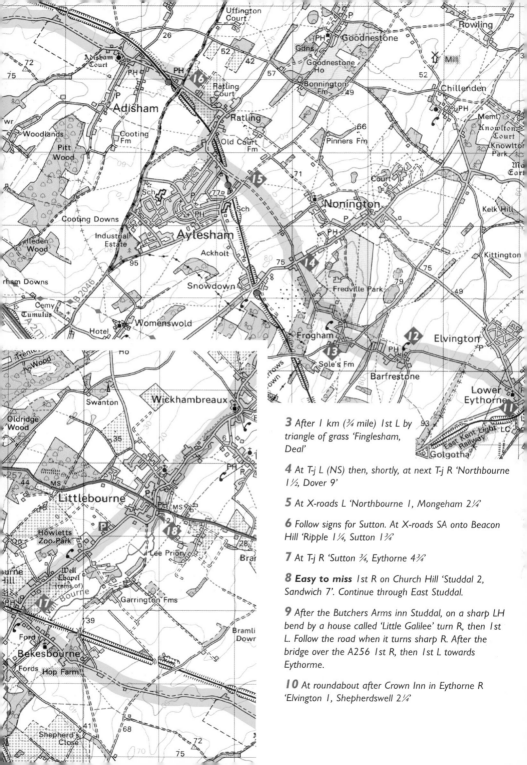

3 After 1 km (¾ mile) 1st L by triangle of grass 'Finglesham, Deal'

4 At T-j L (NS) then, shortly, at next T-j R 'Northbourne 1½, Dover 9'

5 At X-roads L 'Northbourne 1, Mongeham 2¼'

6 Follow signs for Sutton. At X-roads SA onto Beacon Hill 'Ripple 1¼, Sutton 1¾'

7 At T-j R 'Sutton ¾, Eythorne 4¾'

8 **Easy to miss** 1st R on Church Hill 'Studdal 2, Sandwich 7'. Continue through East Studdal.

9 After the Butchers Arms inn Studdal, on a sharp LH bend by a house called 'Little Galilee' turn R, then 1st L. Follow the road when it turns sharp R. After the bridge over the A256 1st R, then 1st L towards Eythorne.

10 At roundabout after Crown Inn in Eythorne R 'Elvington 1, Shepherdswell 2¼'

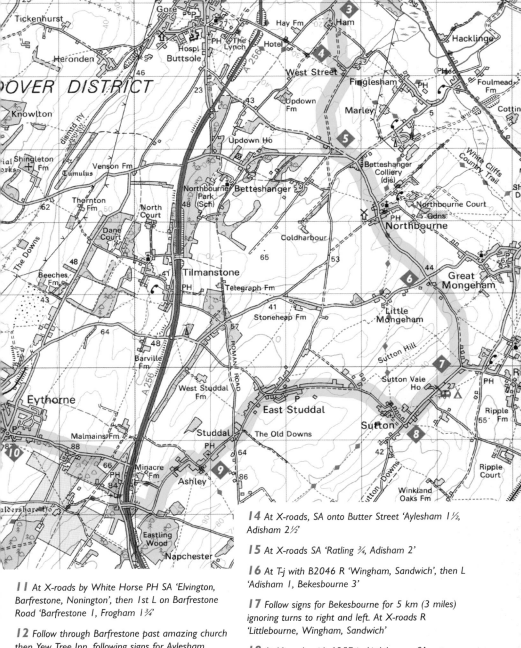

14 At X-roads, SA onto Butter Street 'Aylesham 1½, Adisham 2½'

15 At X-roads SA 'Ratling ¾, Adisham 2'

16 At T-j with B2046 R 'Wingham, Sandwich', then L 'Adisham 1, Bekesbourne 3'

17 Follow signs for Bekesbourne for 5 km (3 miles) ignoring turns to right and left. At X-roads R 'Littlebourne, Wingham, Sandwich'

18 At X-roads with A257 in Littlebourne SA onto Margate Street 'Ickham, Wickhambreaux'

two pages

11 At X-roads by White Horse PH SA 'Elvington, Barfrestone, Nonington', then 1st L on Barfrestone Road 'Barfrestone 1, Frogham 1¾'

12 Follow through Barfrestone past amazing church then Yew Tree Inn, following signs for Aylesham

13 Climb, then descend past Frogham Farm to your right. At start of 2nd hill, by a row of old red-brick cottages R 'Nonington 1, Aylesham 1¾'

Along the Greensand Way south of Godalming

*T*ry this ride just to prove that you do not need to drive down to the South Downs to use your mountain bike! There is a plethora of bridleways in the triangle formed by Godalming, Haslemere and Billingshurst, and this route simply links up a few of them. Why not make up a route of your own by linking up a few others? This is a ride for old footwear and long trousers, which, despite these minor drawbacks, contains some fine views, good climbs and a few surprises.

Hascombe

Nore

Selhurst Common

Nurscombe Farm

Busbridge

120 150   120 120   100   80   90   80   60   120   110

0   5   10

Places of interest

Bramley 8

This village has some attractive buildings including two Lutyens houses, the 16th-century Bramley East Manor in the High Street and some fine Regency and Georgian houses. A 13th-century chancel and the remains of a Norman arch can be seen in Holy Trinity Church.

Hambledon 23

School Cottage, Malthouse Cottage and Malthouse Farm are good examples of 16th- and 17th-century cottages; parts of the church are much older (14th-century) and Court Farm and the Granary are also interesting. The surrounding hills give good views over the downs.

▲ *Woodland track near Hyde stile*

Enton Hall

120 — 130   90   100   130   140   160   160   160   50

15   20   24

1 Facing the White Horse PH, take track to right of it 'Private Road, Hascombe Place Farm'. Continue in same direction beyond farm uphill on bridleway

2 You will soon come to the muddiest section of the ride. The first 100 m (yd) are the worst and there are two more bad stretches in this climb

3 Up and over hill. At T-j by green gate L.

4 After 1½ km (1 mile), at T-j with road R, then 1st L after 800 m (½ mile) on Gate Street. Continue to the end of the tarmac, past farm 'No exit, Keepers only'. Follow in same direction as it becomes single track. (May be muddy, be prepared for nettles)

5 In woodland, by signpost with yellow arrow indicating footpath to the left R, then L following blue arrows

6 Briefly join gravel drive. After 100 m (yd), on RH bend L (in effect SA) uphill on earth track

7 This track joins more major track near house (Bramley Park). Just past house at T-j of tracks L, following wooden fence around

8 At times muddy (nettles). Follow track around Eastwater Barn to tarmac drive by pond. At road L

9 After 1½ km (1 mile), shortly after fine parkland of Thornecombe House on your left R on tarmac drive opposite metal railings 'Public Bridleway'

10 Tarmac turns to track and climbs steeply then more gently. At X-roads of bridleways near top of hill by 4-way signpost SA. At road L past large red-brick tower

11 At T-j with B2130 SA just to the left of Busbridge Parish Council Noticeboard onto dead-end road

12 At T-j at the end of North Munstead Lane R, then at next T-j at the end of Hambledon Road L 'Milford, Eashing'

13 Shortly after passing nursing home on left, opposite Busbridge Lane on right L onto public bridleway

14 Descend to pass between lakes. Climb steeply. At road at the end of the drive to Clock Barn Farm SA 'Public Bridleway, Inwood Cottage'

15 Just before house and 'Private' sign L on track into woodland

16 At road by sign for nurseries R

17 **Easy to miss.** At next T-j SA onto track 'National Trust, Hydon's Ball', then immediately leave main track an turn R onto narrower bridleway

18 Track widens. At X-roads of bridleways SA. At road R then L 'Public Bridleway, Potters Hill'

19 Through farm, across two fairways of the golf course (watch out for golf balls!) in the same direction. At road L

20 Shortly after Enton Hall on left L by pond 'Public bridleway'

21 **Easy to miss.** Follow broad gravel track gently uphill for 800 m (½ mile) passing white gate of Sweetwater Cottage on the right. Just past signpost for Busses Cottage on the right fork L (blue arrow)

22 At times muddy. At road by the Merry Harriers PH R, then after 400 m (yd) 1st L onto Church Lane 'Hambledo Church'

23 Bear R by church through parking area 'Public bridleway'

24 At T-j with broader track R (red arrow), then immediately L steeply uphill onto narrow sunken track. After 200 m (yd) take LH, higher fork (ignore signpost pointing down to the right). This section may be overgrow

25 Follow through woodland then RH edge of field (good views to right). Descend through woodland to road

26 At road R, then L 'Public bridleway'. Follow main track over X-roads of tracks

27 Follow broad gravel track down to small road and turr R. At T-j with B2130 R to return to White Horse PH

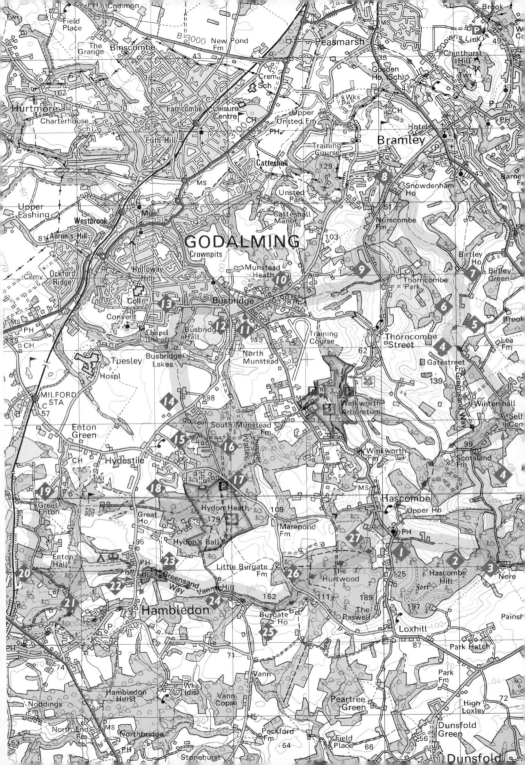

From Buriton onto the western end of the South Downs

This short ride at the western end of the South Downs has all the ingredients of the best routes in the region. The ride starts from a pretty village with a good pub, there is a steep challenging climb through Queen Elizabeth country Park where you may well be tempted away from the main route to explore other waymarked trails and the Visitor Centre. A fast descent leads on to a second good pub at Chalton; the track to the east of the railway line is a slice of bygone England. The second climb through the woods of West Harting Down is on a good stone-based track that can be cycled in all seasons. In addition to all this, fine views from several points along the way, magnificent displays of wild flowers in the spring, changing colours in the autumn and the option of exploring the South Downs Way further east helps you understand the ride's year-round appeal.

Start

The village pond in Buriton, 3 km (2 miles) south of Petersfield

P By the church/pond at the southeast end of Buriton

Distance and grade

21 km (13 miles)

Moderate

Terrain

Quiet lanes, drove roads and woodland tracks. Two main climbs: 122 m (400 ft) from Buriton to the high point in Queen Elizabeth Country Park, 70 m (230 ft) from the B2146 through the woodland of West Harting Down. Lowest point – 70 m (230 ft) at crossing of railway line east of Chalton. Highest point: 201 m (660 ft) at the top of the hill in Queen Elizabeth country Park

Nearest railway

Petersfield, 3 km (2 miles) from the start

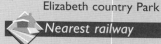

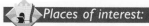
Buriton 1
Sleepy Hampshire village where Edward Gibbon, author of *Decline and Fall of the Roman Empire,* spent his childhood in the Georgian Manor, which is still standing

▲ *The view from Harting Hill with South Harting in the distance*

Queen Elizabeth Country Park 3/4
Walking, cycling, picknicking and grass-skiing in 566 ha (1400 acres) of working countryside, downland and woodlands. There are demonstrations of forest and agricultural activities. There are several waymarked mountain bike rides through the woodlands, starting near the Visitor Centre

Uppark 9 *(just off the route)*
Red-brick Queen Anne mansion overlooking landscaped gardens and South Downs, once home of Emma, Lady Hamilton, Nelson's mistress. The house has recently been restored at great cost after a fire caused major damage

South Harting 10 *(just off the route)*
Village with wide main street lined with 17th-century Georgian houses. There is a slender memorial in the churchyard by sculptor and typographer, Eric Gill

Refreshments

Five Bells PH ❦❦, *Master Robert PH,* **Buriton**
Red Lion PH ❦❦, **Chalton**
Coach & Horses PH, **Compton**
(off the route near instruction 7)

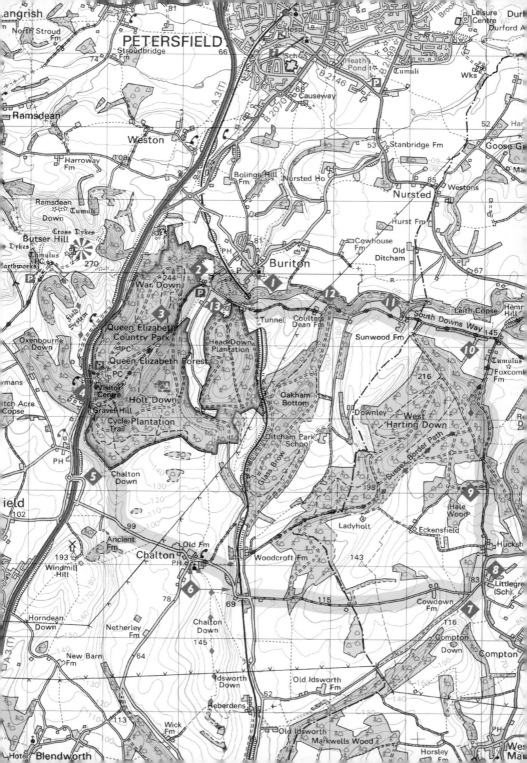

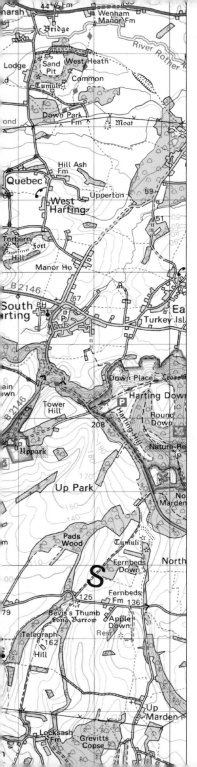

1 From the pond, take South Lane (no through road) 'Hangers Way, Queen Elizabeth Park'

2 Lovely climb on gravel track. Go under a bridge and climb more steeply. At T-j with road at the top of the climb bear R to cross second road and go through car park climbing gently towards wooden gates

3 Climb more steeply. Shortly after the brow of the hill fork L 'South Downs Way. Horses'. Keep climbing and following blue painted posts, horseshoe signs and 'South Downs Way' signs

4 Follow these signs up then down hill over several X-roads of tracks. At a major junction of tracks at the bottom of the hill, with the busy A3 in sight and earshot, turn L onto the lower track along the edge of the woodland, following the red-topped posts

5 Easy to miss. After 1 km (¾ mile), opposite Information Board 15, where the main track swings left, turn R onto a narrow track away from the woodland. At T-j with lane L into Chalton

6 At the triangle of grass just before the Red Lion PH turn L 'Ditcham, Idsworth, Compton'. Climb then fast descent. 100 m (yd) after crossing the railway bridge, on a RH bend, SA onto broad stone track

7 Lovely section. Go past farm and onto tarmac. At T-j with lane by black metal lamplights turn L. At T-j with B2146 L 'Petersfield, Harting'

8 After 600 m (yd) on RH bend, bear L onto broad stone track 'Bridleway'

9 At X-roads with major track shortly after green metal gate SA towards grey metal gate 'Bridleway'

10 Beautiful wooded section. **Easy to miss.** The track turns to tarmac. Shortly after red-brick cottages on the left and a house called 'Downlands' on the right, take the next track L

11 At T-j with tarmac L 'South Downs Way'

12 Ignore right turn on 'Cart Track'. Follow the tarmac as it swings left 'South Downs Way', then swings right and turns to track as it passes beneath power lines

13 Track becomes tarmac. Immediately before a triangle of grass by the road junction turn R, Hangers Way 'Bridleway', onto a narrow track to rejoin outward route and return to the start

3 Glorious downland riding near Goodwood

The ride takes in some of the very best scenery at the western end of the South Downs. Each of the five climbs is rewarded with either great views, a great descent or both. There is a satisfying mixture of woodland and open downland and the opportunity to stop at one or two of the excellent pubs on the way. You may even get a chance to race against the horses at Goodwood if you turn up on a race day!

Start

The car park 3 km (2 miles) south of Singleton off the A286 on the west side of St Roche's Hill

P As above

Distance and grade

37 km (23 miles)

Moderate/strenuous

Terrain

Five climbs of between 122 and 137 m (400 and 450 feet), some pushing required; downs and woodland

Nearest railway

Fishbourne, 6½ km (4 miles) south of the route at Kingley Vale Nature Reserve or Petersfield, 10 km (6 miles) west of North Marden

1 From car park cross road onto track. At fork by ruined house bear L away from the woodland on the right and along the field edge on fine gentle descent

2 Through gate into open field. Bear slightly L downhill. Through gate in same direction towards road and houses

3 At T-j with A286 R, then L 'Binderton Lane'

4 At B2141 R, then L on bridleway

➡ three pages

20 At A286 SA onto track 'South Downs Way'

21 **Easy to miss.** Climb to top of hill, go past hut on stilts and trig point on your left and through X-roads of footpaths. 400 m (¼ mile) past the brow of the hill at 4-way signpost turn R onto grassy track at right angles to South Downs Way downhill into wood.

22 At X-roads with forestry track SA. At T-j with next forestry track R 'Public Bridleway'

23 Follow major track to X-roads. Turn L 'Petworth 10, East Dean 1'

24 Just past Fox PH R towards telephone box, then L at triangle of grass

25 Climb steadily for 1½ km (1 mile) on major track past racecourse to road. At road R

26 Follow racecourse on right. At T-j R 'Singleton 2, Midhurst 8', then L opposite grandstand '6 Label Only'

27 Follow track to the left of iron railings. At gate SA into open field, contouring to join better defined track and to return to start

Stoke Down Stoughton Telegraph Hill North Marden Hooks

180
80 100 80 110 120 160 130 110 140

0   5   10   15

CHICHESTER DISTRICT

West Dean Gardens 3

These informal gardens are slightly off the route. Within the 30 acres are a gazebo, a pergola, some outstanding trees, a spring garden, a wild garden and a walled garden.

The Mardens 14-18

North (17), East (nr.18), Up (nr.15) and West (nr.14) Marden are connected by lanes twisting between the fields and woods; a very peaceful area.

Compton 15

Lying in a wooded valley a little off the route, Compton consists of a few attractive cottages, a church, a pub and a shop.

5 Follow this track for 2 km (1¼ miles) over X-roads of bridleways. At sign for Kingley Vale follow the wood on your right closely, turning R uphill to follow wood edge 'Nature Conservancy. National Nature Reserve. Kingley Vale'

6 At fork in clearing L along edge of fence

7 At fork in very gloomy stretch of woodland R on the steeper uphill track. At next fork R uphill with wood close to the right

8 After brow of hill, by breeze block base take main track into wood for superb descent

9 At road R, then 1st L towards telephone box. At fork bear L 'Public Bridleway'

10 Steep climb. Fork L along edge of wood. Descend to road

11 At road SA. At fork after 200 m (yd) R very steeply uphill

12 Follow main track until reaching sharp bend in major well-made track with sign for 'Lye Common, No Riding' to your right. Turn L.

13 At road R

14 After 1 km (¾ mile), shortly after sharp LH bend in road by a large square house R onto track by double metal gate

15 Follow main track with wood on right. This track becomes narrow with hedgerow on left. Follow towards house and trees on top of Telegraph Hill and take main track to road

16 At T-j with road R following signs for North Marden. At T-j L 'North Marden'

17 At T-j with B2141 R 'Chichester 8½'. At top of hill L 'Royal Oak PH', 'Hooksway ¼'

18 Once past PH take middle of three tracks

19 Join the South Downs Way. Climb out of woods, past trig point then a fast descent to the road

 three pages

▲ Goodwood House

West from Amberley on the South Downs Way over Bignor Hill to East Dean

Terrain

A long, at times steep, climb of 228 m (750 ft) from Amberley to the masts beyond Bignor Hill, a climb of 85 m (280 ft) from the A285 to the X-roads with the South Downs Way, and one of 115 m (380 ft) from Droke Forestry Car Park to just below the masts

A kill-or-cure climb at the start of this ride takes you from sea level at the tidal River Arun near Amberley up over Bignor Hill, with the views opening up behind you with each revolution of the pedals (any excuse for a stop!). The route leaves the South Downs Way near the car park on Bignor Hill because the climb on the other side of the A285 is through a ploughed field. Broaden your horizons – there are numerous bridlepaths to be explored either side of the South Downs Way. Once you have arrived at Tegleaze, to the west of the A285, prepare for a magnificent descent into East Dean. There is a chance to refuel before you climb through the woods and follow the ridge west back to the roundabout by the A284. A very fast road descent should get rid of most of the mud on your bike!

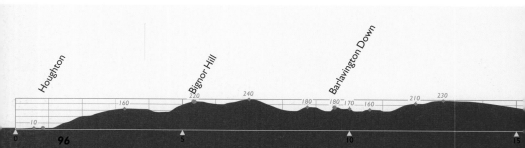

Arundel 19
The great Norman castle is quite a long way
south of the route but Arundel Park is nearer.
There is a large Wildfowl Trust reserve with
exotic swans, geese and ducks.

 Off-road riding tips

- Padded shorts and gloves make off-road
  riding more comfortable

- If there is any possibility of rain, take
  something waterproof. Never
  underestimate the effects of wind-chill
  when you are wet, even in summer

  - In wet and cold conditions, keep a
    layer of warm clothes next to the
    skin – thermal underwear or wool

  - After fixing a puncture, check the
    inside of the tyre for embedded
    thorns before replacing the inner
    tube. A screwdriver is useful for win-
    kling out difficult thorns

  - If your brake blocks look as though
    they are wearing thin, take a spare set
    with you. New brake blocks are much
    cheaper than new rims

- Take a compass with you for crossing
  moorland or when there is poor visibility
  and know how to use it

Refreshments

Bridge Inn ●, Black Horse PH ●, *Boat
House PH, Cafe,* **Amberley**
Hurdlemakers PH ●, **East Dean**
George and Dragon PH ●●,
Houghton *Tea stop at* **car park near
A29 A284 roundabout**

East Dean

Droke

Houghton

160

210

200

240

100

110

20

25

97 30

31

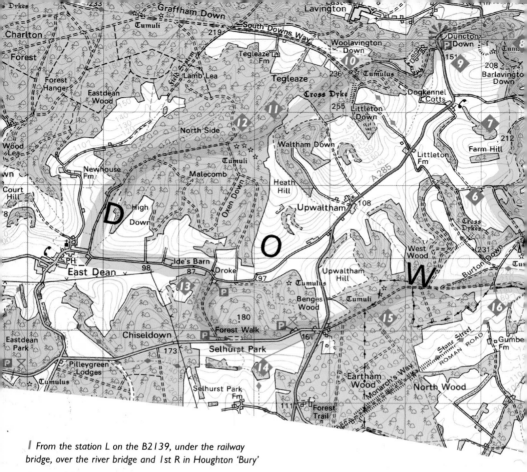

1 From the station L on the B2139, under the railway bridge, over the river bridge and 1st R in Houghton 'Bury'

2 After 400 m (¼ mile) L on track 'South Downs Way'

3 Steep climb. At T-j with A29 R, then L on continuation of South Downs Way

4 Follow South Downs Way, just past barn, dog-leg L then R, steeply uphill over Bignor Hill to car park/end of tarmac road/sign with Latin names

5 Through car park, following South Downs Way signs through wooden barrier ('No cars'). After 100 m (yd), leave South Downs Way and bear R uphill on broad stony track ('Public bridleway') towards, then to the right of masts

6 **Easy to miss.** Go past patch of woodland to the right then a field. Just **before** start of second patch of woodland, leave the main track and turn R 'Public Bridleway' following the wire fence on the right. Shortly, at 3-way split take LH track

7 Follow in same direction. Descend to go beneath power lines carried by telegraph poles, then climb towards wood on hill (maybe overgrown)

8 On the descent in the wood at a fork by a signpost L 'Public bridleway', then shortly, at T-j with more major track (3-way signpost) L uphill

9 Exit wood, cross field. At road R then L 'Duncton Quarrying'. Just before gate to quarry L uphill on broad chalk path

10 At X-roads with South Downs Way by a large wooden post with 'Tegleaze' written on it SA 'East Dean'

11 Cross clearing on grassy track. Through gate onto stony track. 100 m (yd) after rejoining woodland on right, just before the main track ends at a gate into a field R on smaller track into forest

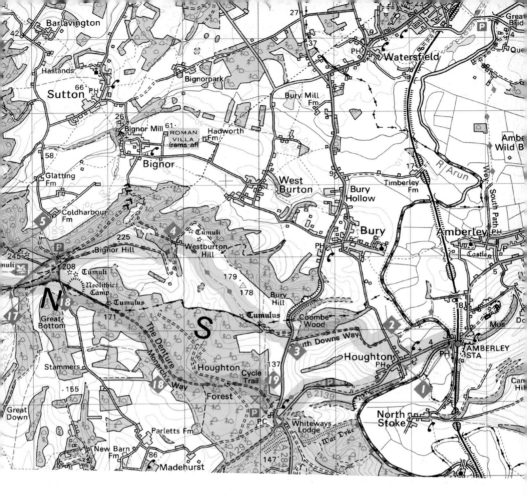

12 At major X-roads of forestry tracks SA downhill on long straight track

13 At road L (or R for PH/stores). After 1½ km (1 mile), at a car park by Forestry Commission sign for 'Droke Forest' R uphill on gravel track into wood

14 At road L. At T-j with A285 by St Mary's Farm SA 'Public bridleway'

15 Woodland climb, then through clearing and along RH edge of woodland with fine views to right

16 At major fork of tracks at the edge of the woodland you have been following on your left, with the masts diagonally uphill to your left, SA 'Public Bridleway' along the LH edge of woodland

17 At X-roads of bridleways, with a large field to your right, SA into woodland 'Public Bridleway'. At junction with more major track SA 'Public Bridleway'

18 At next X-roads, near a wooden bench and a National Trust sign for Bignor Hill SA with field to left and wood to right. Good descent through woodland then clearing, bearing L at the bottom of the clearing

19 At major forestry X-roads SA to arrive at Whiteways Picnic Site. At roundabout L on B2139 'Amberley, Storrington' for a fast road descent to return to Amberley

5 East from Amberley over Wepham Down and Rackham Hill

*T*here is a lot of breezy, open downland on this ride and the fine views one expects (and deserves) from the top of the ridges. The ride starts with a steep road climb, followed by a descent into and climb out of a steep valley (can you do it without getting off?). The route continues down into the quiet tucked-away village of Burpham, which has a fine pub. A woodland stretch follows, leaving the trees just as the going starts to get muddy. The section above Lower Barpham is wonderful, perched right on the edge of the very steep hillside. As you continue to climb, views open up on both sides before the descent to Lee Farm. A final climb onto Rackham Hill gives views over the Arun Valley and sets you up for the last descent.

 Start

Railway station at Amberley

P As above

 Distance and grade

24 km (15 miles)

Moderate/strenuous

 Terrain

Three major climbs: 100 m (330 ft) from Amberley to Downs Farm, 143 m (470 ft) from Burpham to Barpham Hill and 109 m (360 ft) from Lee Farm to Rackham Hill

Nearest railway

Amberle

 Refreshments

Bridge Inn 🍺, Black Horse PH 🍺, Boat House PH, cafe, **Amberley** George and Dragon PH 🍺🍺, **Burpham**

The Burgh — Peppering High Barn — Burpham

Burpham 6

A hamlet with brick and flint thatched cottages and a Norman church overlooking the water-meadows.

Off-road riding tips

- Lower your saddle when going down steep off-road sections, keep the pedals level, stand up out of the saddle to let your legs absorb the bumps and keep your weight over the rear wheel

- If using a jet spray to clean your bike, do not aim the hose directly at the hubs or bottom bracket but clean these parts from above

- Lubricate your bike after washing it or after a very wet ride, paying particular attention to the chain

- Carry a water bottle in the bottle carrier and keep it filled, particularly on hot days

- Good energy foods that do not take up much space are dates, figs, dried fruit and nuts

- Good equipment does not make you a good cyclist. The only bad cyclists are those who show no consideration to others, whether by weaving around, failing to indicate or riding on pavements in on-road situations, or by failing to follow the countryside code, and showing no respect to walkers and horseriders when off-road

- Always take a few coins for emergencies

- Make sure there is nothing loose and dangling (laces, daypack straps, pannier straps) that may get caught in the spokes, chain or pedals

Springhead Hill

Rackham Hill

140

190

190

190

190

15

20

24

1 Out of car park R, then after 800 m (½ mile) 1st R on High Titten. Climb on tarmac towards round storage bins

2 Just before large round storage bins L on track 'No vehicles except access'. Continue past farm buildings. At fork take RH, lower track (**not** South Downs Way), then after 100 m (yd) R at next fork

3 On descent, at fork bear R to stay close to the fence on your right. Descend into the valley and climb steeply

4 Through gate. At T-j of tracks at top of hill by a 4-way signpost R then 100 m (yd) before farm buildings L sharply back on yourself

5 On broad track past farm and onto tarmac. 1st R by triangle of grass (NS), then 1st L opposite Peppering Farm passing The Garden House on your right

6 Past George and Dragon PH, then on sharp LH bend 1st R

7 At T-j in Wepham R, then L on concrete track 'Public bridleway'

8 Climb steeply on concrete track. At top of hill on sharp LH bend bear R (in effect SA) 'Public bridleway'

9 At T-j of tracks at the bottom by sign for Angmering Park Estate R, then at fork L. At X-roads by tarmac road L towards farm buildings (this detour avoids a very steep, muddy climb)

10 Ignore 1st bridleway to the left by gate and Angmering Park Estate sign. At X-roads of tracks bear slightly L on broad forestry track (ignore the footpath signposted to the right). After 1 km (¾ mile) bear R, staying on main track

11 At X-roads with tarmac by red-brick Keepers Cottage SA. After 1 km (¾ mile), at fork of tracks L, following fence round

12 May be muddy. At green gate L onto track with fabulous views to the right

13 Emerge out of wood via red gate. SA main stony track. Continue uphill in same direction through double wooden gates and take the RH fork

14 Through field with fine views left and right, towards and through next set of double wooden gates. Grassy descent. At T-j with broad track R

15 Past farm. At barn at bottom of hill, on RH bend L uphill through double metal gates

16 Climb steadily for 2 km (1¼ miles) 106 m (350 feet) climb). At T-j at the top L. Follow signs for South Downs Way for 5½ km (3½ miles) back into Amberley

North of Worthing: Cissbury Ring to the Adur Valley and Chanctonbury

Findon is one of those small but perfectly formed villages for cyclists: two pubs, a tea shop, a shop open seven days a week, even a bike shop! The route climbs towards Cissbury Ring, a massive Iron Age hill fort on the site of Neolithic flint mines. This route passes below Cissbury Ring, but if you do visit it, please follow the waymarks and do not stray from the bridleways. The route continues over downland towards the impressive architecture of Lancing College. A road section along the Adur Valley provides resting time before the major climb via the South Downs Way to Chanctonbury Ring. Sadly, this magnificent copse of beech trees was savaged by the great gale of 1987, but the views remain spectacular.

 Start

Car park by village green, Findon

P Near village green or on Stable Lane, Findon or in car park beneath Cissbury Ring if there is no space in Findon (join route at instruction 4)

 Distance and grade

26 km (16 miles)

Moderate/strenuous

 Terrain

Two climbs: 76 m (250 ft) from Findon to Cissbury Ring and almost 240 m (800 ft) from the Adur Valley to Chanctonbury Ring

Nearest railway

Lancing, 2½ km (1½ miles) from the route at its southeast corner

 Refreshments

Village House Hotel, Gun Inn 🍺, Green Welly cafe and tea shop, **Findon**

Steep Down

140
60
90
110
100
20

0
5
10

Places of interest

St Mary's, Bramber 11

This well-preserved timbered house was built in around 1470 and has some fine panelled rooms. The 'Painted Room' is particularly well-known and was decorated for a visit of Elizabeth I.

Steyning 12-13

This small town is slightly off the route but has some interesting old buildings including a Norman church with nave and chancel arch, a tiled Market House with a clock turret, a medieval poor-house and some 15th-century houses along the High Street.

Chanctonbury Ring 13

There are excellent views over the countryside from these prehistoric earthworks. The fort is well-known for the trees planted within its walls.

Off-road riding tips

- Keep some spare dry clothes and shoes in the car to change into and carry some bin liners in the car to put dirty, wet clothes in

- Keep other possessions dry in very wet weather by carrying them in two sets of plastic bags

- Experiment with saddle height, forwards and backwards adjustment of saddle, tilt of saddle up or down and height of the handlebars (do not exceed maximum height) until you find your most comfortable riding position

- Anticipate hills by changing into the right gear before it gets tough

- If there is an easier gear when struggling up a hill, use it, and let the bike do the work, not your knee joints

- Alter your starting point to take account of the wind direction so that you are not cycling back into the wind when you are tired

- If there is any possibilty of cycling in twilight or darkness, take lights with you. As a precaution in winter, take a reflective belt

Bottolphs

Chanctonbury

190   230   110   90   23(

15   20   15   26

1 From Village Green L on Stable Lane 'Chanctonbury, Unsuitable for motors'

2 At sign for Gallops Farm, 'Private Road', R uphill on track

3 Climb steadily on broad chalk and flint track, passing white house on the left. At top of hill at major X-roads of tracks R towards Cissbury Ring, following wooden fence

4 At T-j just beneath Cissbury (National Trust sign) L downhill on broad stony track

5 At major X-roads of tracks SA towards pylon on horizon

6 At X-roads with road near Sompting sign SA

7 At X-roads of tracks near pylon R to go under lines

8 Keep bearing L along fence on left Join tarmac briefly, bear L along fence

9 As road swings sharp right go SA onto track past cottage 'Public Bridleway'

10 At T-j with tarmac at bottom of hill R. After 150 m (yd) by light-coloured house L. At 3rd T-j (traffic lights to the right) turn L

11 After 5 km (3 miles) on road, in Annington while climbing hill, shortly after Annington House rear entrance on right, on sharp RH bend turn L onto track 'South Downs Way'

12 Follow signs for South Downs Way to road. R then after 800 m (½ mile) L on continuation of South Downs Way

13 Follow South Downs Way signs for 4 km (2½ miles) as far as trig point beyond Chanctonbury Ring. Where South Downs Way turns sharply right, continue L downhill

14 Fast descent. At X-roads of tracks L

15 After 800 m (½ mile), after bottom of hill as climb begins, just past house on left, R on concrete track. At road SA through bridlegate diagonally L across field

16 At gate at edge of field SA uphill with wood on left, past farm. Concrete/tarmac track to return to Findon

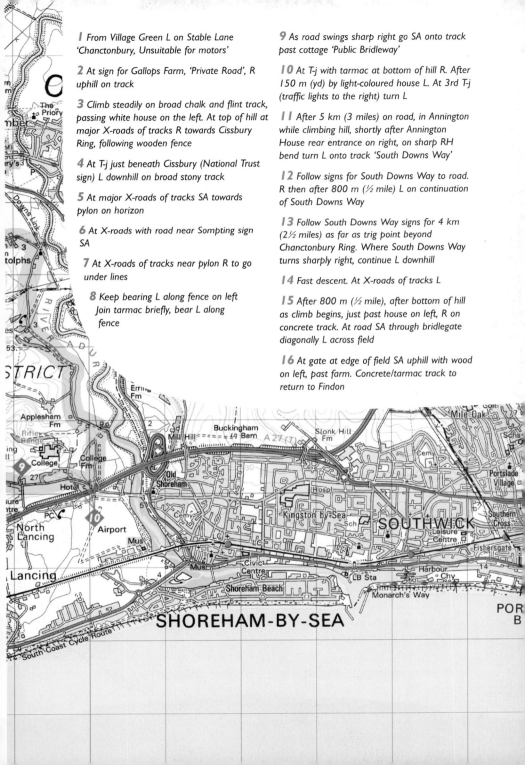

West from Alfriston over the Downs to Firle Beacon

Alfriston is a honey pot for tourists arriving by the coachload; but have no fear: this ride escapes quickly onto the Downs where the coaches cannot go. A long steady climb on the South Downs Way brings you to the ridge with magnificent views back across the Cuckmere Valley and down across the Sussex Weald. At times it is hard to believe that you are in the densely populated southeast of England with such big open spaces and views all around. A fast descent via Norton and Bishopstone, with a little negotiation of a housing development, brings you to the start of the second climb. Dodge those golf balls as you make your way across the golf course back onto the ridge for the final swoop into Alfriston.

Refreshments

Star PH 🍺🍺, lots of choice in **Alfriston**
Ram PH 🍺🍺, **West Firle** (almost
150 m (500 ft) height loss)

Start

The square, Alfriston

🅿 Long-term car park in Alfriston (turn up early) or turn R opposite George Inn and park in 'Kings Ride leading to Broadway' or some parking on the track at the top end of the village (instruction 2)

Distance and grade

21 km (13 miles)

🗲🗲🗲🗲

Moderate/strenuous

Terrain

Two climbs: 198 m (650 ft) from Alfriston to Firle Beacon, 161 m (530 ft) from Norton and Bishopstone back onto the South Downs Way

Nearest railway

Newhaven or Bishopstone, both 2½ km (1½ miles) from the southeast corner of the route, or Berwick, 5 km (3 miles) north of Alfriston

Alfriston 1

Timbered houses with overhanging storeys line the main street. The large church dominating the green was built out of flint in the shape of a Greek Cross.

▲ *The South Downs Way near Alfriston*

Next to the church is the half-timbered Clergy House, which was the first building ever to be acquired by the National Trust. It was built for a community of parish priests in 1350 and contains large dining and recreation areas and some smaller rooms; it now houses an exhibition on 'Wealden House Building'. The ancient and interesting Market Cross Inn (once a smugglers' haunt), Star Inn and George Inn are worth visiting.

Alfriston Heritage Centre and Blacksmith's Museum 1

15th-century buildings contain the old forge, a blacksmith's and farrier's museum. The history of Alfriston is displayed in an annexe.

Firle Place 4

Built in the 16th century, this house was extensively altered between 1713 and 1754. The south side gable and the two courtyards of the original plan survived but most of the house was swallowed up by the new one. Upstairs, there are fine collections of 18th-century French furniture, Sevres porcelain and some important pictures. The long gallery (built in 1713) overlooks the South Downs and contains interesting works of the English School including David Teniers's 'The Wine Harvest'.

Norton

Bishopstone

20 50 100 180 210

15 20 21

1 From the square, facing tea shop and antiques shop L

2 After 1 km (¾ mile) at the top of steady climb at X-roads with Winton Street L on broad track

3 At 3-way fork take middle or LH track uphill. At X-roads at top R on South Downs Way

4 Follow South Downs Way for 5½ km (3½ miles) over Firle Beacon towards masts. At car park just before masts L on tarmac road

5 Through farm. Steep descent. Through bridlegate and continue along valley bottom. Follow track as it swings to the right. Climb for 300 m (yd) then at 4-way signpost turn L

6 At X-roads of tracks at the end of the field on your left L downhill towards houses

7 Track becomes tarmac. Bear R at triangle of grass, pass through Norton, descend then climb. At brow of hill in Bishopstone with a row of flint cottages ahead, turn L onto broad track 'Public Bridleway, East Blatchington'

8 Take RH fork after 200 m (yd) then bear R around RH edge of field alongside stone wall. At T-j with road L

9 After 800 m (½ mile), at the start of housing estate, by the first street light and a sign for 'Grand Avenue' R down tarmac path. At road SA on continuation of path to emerge at Pilgrims School.

10 At T-j by school L towards no through road. Just by sign for Seaford Golf Club bear L on bridleway 'Bo Peep 3 miles'

11 Through gate onto golf course. Aim to the R of the green and you will soon discover a track climbing to the L between hedgerows

12 Follow this uphill over X-roads with concrete track. At junction of tracks at clearing at top of hill SA through bridlegate (blue arrow)

13 Down then up, following the track in the same direction towards the white post at the end of the big field (stick close to fence on right)

14 Rejoin South Downs Way, turning R along ridge to return to Alfriston. At X-roads of tracks above Alfriston either SA on South Downs Way or L to return by outward route

8 East from Alfriston via Friston Forest to Jevington and Windover Hill

Be prepared for the hordes of tourists in Alfriston. You will soon leave them behind as you climb steeply towards the top of Lullington Heath and are rewarded with fine views of the impressive valley between Lullington Heath and Windover Hill. A stretch in Friston Forest takes you as far as a vineyard in Westdean. The views have been good, but better still await you from the top of Willingdon Hill, with the English Channel away to the southeast. Jevington has a pub, but its famous chalk figure, The Long Man, lies on the Downs on the route back towards Alfriston.

Refreshments

Star PH ●●, lots of choice in **Alfriston**
Eight Bells PH, **Jevington**

Start

The square, Alfriston

 Long-term car park in Alfriston (turn up early) or turn R opposite George Inn and park on 'Kings Ride leading to Broadway'; or use car parks in or near Exceat and join ride at Westdean

Distance and grade

24 km (15 miles)

Moderate/strenuous

Terrain

Three climbs: 122 m (400 ft) from Alfriston to Lullington Heath, 161 m (530 ft) from Friston to the top of Willingdon Hill, 100 m (330 ft) from Jevington to Windover Hill

Nearest railway

Berwick Station, 5 km (3 miles) north of Alfriston

Drusillas 1
Slightly off the route to the north, Drusillas is a zoo park with large collections of such animals as llamas, monkeys and penguins. There is also an adventure playground, a tropical butterfly house and a miniature railway.

Lullington and Litlington 4
These pretty villages have interesting churches: Lullington's is the smallest in England and is really just a chancel left from an older church; Litlington's is very old, dating back to about 1150.

The Living World, Seven Sisters Country Park 7
This is an exotic natural history exhibition where all the exhibits are alive. The displays change according to the season but include praying mantids, tarantulas, giant silk moths and fresh water aquaria. The Country Park contains some beautiful scenery.

Seven Sisters Sheep Centre 10
The practicalites of working with sheep throughout the year are demonstrated here and there are exhibitions on the history of Downland sheep. Processes in wool spinning and sheep yoghurt and cheese making are also displayed.

Friston and East Dean 10
St Mary's Church at Friston used to be a landmark for smugglers. The church in East Dean houses an unusual copy of a Norman font.

Jevington

190   180   190   180   190
90
15   20   24

1 Facing the tea shop and antiques' shop in the square R towards the A27, then 1st R 'Lullington ¾, Litlington 1¼'

2 Follow signs for Litlington. At T-j by large black wooden barn R 'Litlington, Seaford', then 1st L on track just past a letter box on your right 'Jevington 2½ miles'

3 Climb on broad track. At T-j with another major track bear L. At top by stone pillar with plaque for 'Lullington Heath' R 'Charleston Bottom' (directions are on the side of wooden post)

4 Fast descent. At junction of six tracks at the bottom of the valley ignore 1st right along valley floor, take next R steeply uphill on stony track 'Snap Hill'

5 Steep climb. At next junction SA 'Friston, Westdean'

6 At next major junction R on straight, broad, grassy track slightly downhill. After 800 m (½ mile) fork R off main track 'Westdean' (blue arrow)

7 Through clearing, then back into woodland to join better stone-based forestry track. Follow this main track as it swings L uphill and completes a 180 degree turn

8 Climb, then descend on broad stone-based track. As it swings sharp left with a large clearing to the left bear R downhill onto chalk/grass track into woodland. Follow in same direction down then steeply up and along RH field edge towards tower. At T-j with tarmac with flint house ahead L

9 Follow this lane as it swings right and climbs. At T-j with road at exit of Friston Forest turn R

10 Near the brow of the hill, before joining the A259, just by the sign for 'Friston' sharply L 'Old Willingdon Rd'

11 Steady climb, fabulous views. At T-j at top of hill with flint barn ruins ahead turn L. At X-roads with South Downs Way by stone marker SA. Just before car park sharp L almost back on yourself through bridlegate 'Bridleway, Jevington 1¼ miles' (**not** the obvious broad chalk track which is the Weald Way)

12 Long grassy descent and short woodland section into Jevington. At T-j at the end of Willingdon Lane, opposite flint cottages R

13 300 m (yd) after Eight Bells PH on your left, opposite Old Post Office L onto Green Lane 'No Through Road'

14 Ignore Weald Way to the right . Track becomes sunken lane beneath a canopy of trees. At fork R then shortly join South Downs Way and bear R. Fork R in a clearing following South Downs Way signs for 4 km (2½ miles). At T-j with road SA

15 At T-j with road at bottom of hill by triangle of grass bear R (in effect SA) 'Alfriston'. Cross river. At next T-j L 'Alfriston ½, Seaford 5'

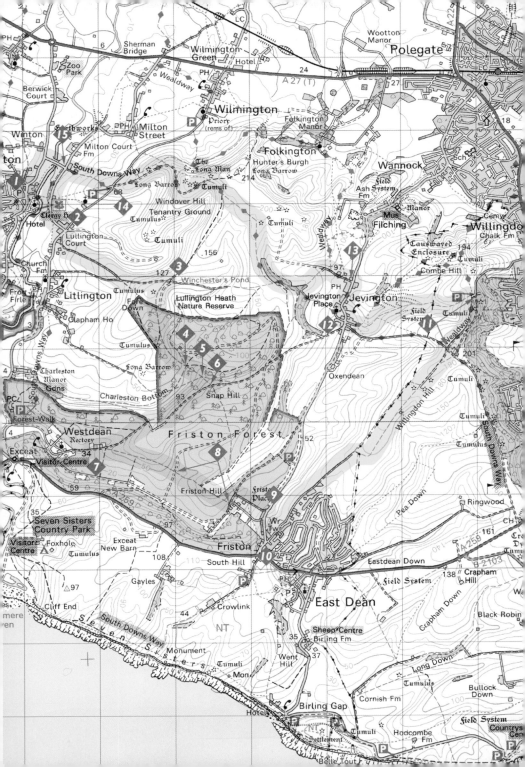

9 From Wye onto the North Downs to northeast of Ashford

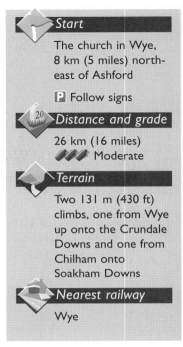

Start

The church in Wye, 8 km (5 miles) north-east of Ashford

P Follow signs

Distance and grade

26 km (16 miles)
/// Moderate

Terrain

Two 131 m (430 ft) climbs, one from Wye up onto the Crundale Downs and one from Chilham onto Soakham Downs

Nearest railway

Wye

The ride wastes no time in getting onto the North Downs Way as it climbs away from the delights of Wye onto the Crundale Downs. There is a particularly lovely section through the woods on a recently improved length of bridleway. If you come across any muddy sections elsewhere on this route, write to the local authority (Rights of Way Department), citing the improved stretch as an example of what the paths should be like. A short road section takes you past Sole Street and into Forestry Commission woodland. The smell that may soon have you wrinkling your nostrils comes from a glue factory in the middle of nowhere. Descend to Chilham for a wide range of temptations, then climb again onto the North Downs Way, a joy to follow with its distinctive waymarking.

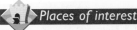

Withersdane Gardens 1
Created in the grounds of the Victorian Withersdane Hall, now part of London University, these gardens were designed for teaching purposes. Among the unusual plants found here are pittosporum, trumpet vines and New Zealand flax. The paulownia tree is probably the largest in the country. The herb and pool gardens are best in early summer, the rose garden and main borders are best in mid- to late summer.

Refreshments

New Flying Horse PH 🍺, *Tickled Trout PH* 🍺, *lots of choice in* **Wye**
Compasses PH 🍺, **Sole Street**
Woolpack PH 🍺, *White Horse PH* 🍺🍺, *tea shops,* **Chilham**

Godmersham 26
Slightly off the route and surrounded by parkland, Godmersham is a tiny village. The interesting Palladian house, which stands in landscaped gardens overlooking the Stour Valley, was owned by Edward Knight whose sister Jane Austen frequently stayed here. There is a monument to him in the flint church, which has a Norman tower and chancel.

Julliberrie Downs

Mountain Street

Boughton Corner

130   160   80   170

60   60   60   30

15   20   25   26

1 With your back to the church, facing the main street L out of town, then 1st L by telephone box on Olantigh Road 'Crundale'

2 After 200 m (yd), opposite the penultimate red-brick college building R on Occupation Road 'Public Bridleway, North Downs Way'

3 At road SA 'Public bridleway, North Downs Way'

4 Steeply uphill into woodland. At road R

5 At top of hill SA through gate 'Sheep. All dogs on leads', 'No parking'. Follow SA towards wood, through gate and L along edge of wood

6 Follow edge of field gently downhill. Join a wider track. At bottom of decent through woodland, with a gate opening into field ahead R onto track through woodland (blue arrow)

7 At X-roads wlth concrete track SA

8 At farm buildings bear L on major track uphill (not marked on map)

9 After a very steep section, as gradient eases just past metal gate sharply L back on yourself (blue arrow)

10 Lovely woodland track, then downland with good views

11 At T-j with road by church R downhill, then steeply uphill

12 At T-j L, then after 400 m (yd) 1st R on track

13 At the end of broad track by a field gate R along edge of woodland (**not** yellow arrow)

14 Along the edge of the wood, then field, then into the next wood on a more major track, following in the same direction on ever-improving surface

15 At T-j with road by Forestry Commission sign 'Denge Wood' L

16 Shortly after passing two brick houses and the glue factory with chimneys on your left, on RH bend go L into wood 'Public Bridleway' on a stone waymark. At fork of tracks at start of wood L on less distinct track

17 At field SA, following line of telegraph poles

18 Through two gates across field in same direction towards wood, crossing beneath telephone wires and through bridlegate

19 At the corner of wood, follow field edge on faint track along LH edge of wood. At the corner of the field follow track into wood, following blue arrows. Take the major track down to tarmac and turn L

20 At T-j with road on sharp bend, L on track 'Byway, Stour Valley Walk'

21 **Easy to miss.** Follow this track for 2½ km (1½ miles) ignoring turnings. At X-roads of tracks by wooden post with blue and yellow arrows and logo for Stour Valley Walk, with double wooden gates 20 m (yd) to your left and a less well-defined, grassier track ahead, follow main track R downhill

22 At main road (A28) R, then 1st L opposite lay-by. At T-j at the end of Branch Road L

23 In square, with entrance to castle ahead L, then at T-j R (in effect SA) 'No Through Road'

24 After 1½ km (1 mile), as road bears left to Hurst Farm SA onto woodland track 'No cars, motorbikes except access', 'North Downs Way'

25 Follow main track as it turns R uphill, then L near top of hill, following signs for 'North Downs Way'

26 From here onwards for 4 km (2½ miles) follow the red arrows indicating the North Downs Way as far as Soakham Farm, then the road

27 At road L. At offset X-roads with A28 SA 'Wye, Brook, Hastingleigh'

28 After railway crossing 1st L 'Car Park' to return to church

On the North Downs above the Elham Valley, north of Folkestone

A short, easy ride on top of the eastern end of the North Downs near Folkestone starts with a climb through woodland and alternates quiet lanes with off-road sections through out its length.

Warning

There are two sections on this route that are prone to get muddy, between instructions 9 & 10 and between 11 & 12. Be prepared to find road alternatives

Refreshments

*Endeavour PH, **Wootton***
*Kings Arms PH ●, **Elham***
*Jackdaw PH, **Denton***
Otherwise, make detour to
Swingfield Street** or **Densole

Start

The Endeavour PH, Wootton, 13 km (8 miles) north of Folkestone, just off the A260

P You may park in the pub car park **only** if you are going to use the pub. Please do not abuse this. There is limited car parking near the village hall in Wootton. Otherwise, park your car in Densole and join the route at instruction 10, or in Elham and join the route at instruction 17 at Rake shole Farm

Distance and grade

19 km (12 miles)
Easy/moderate

Terrain

The ride is on top of the Downs, so there are no major climbs. The steepest is the last one back up the hill to Wootton

Nearest railway

Shepherdswell, 5 km (3 miles) north east of Wootton

Densole

130   150

0   5

The Butterfly Centre, Swingfield 8

A large greenhouse contains an exhibition explaining the life-cycle of butterflies. There is also an area for British butterflies, a landscaped garden and many tropical plants.

▲ Reindeer Wood near Densole

1 With your back to the pub R 'Geddinge, Shepherdswell'

2 At the bottom of the hill opposite a sign for Eythorne and Shepperdswell on your left R onto track through woodland

3 At concrete track by barn bear R

4 At T-j with road L 'Selsted ¾, Lydden 4, Folkestone 6'

5 At T-j L 'Swingfield, Lydden, Dover'

6 At next T-j R 'Swingfield 1, Folkestone 6'

7 Shortly after a left turning to Swingfield Street, on RH bend, bear L (in effect SA) (NS)

8 After sharp RH bend by houses, just before mast L onto track. Horseshoe sign

9 Continue in same direction, ignoring turnings and crossing several X-roads at right angles until reaching A260 (the last section may be muddy, in which case turn R off track to join A260, which runs parallel)

10 At T-j with A260 L, then 1st R just after sign for Hawkinge onto Pay Street

11 After 800 m (½ mile), opposite 1st turning on right L onto track

12 This is muddy at the end. Join tarmac. At X-roads with road R, then 1st R just after Cat and Custard Pot PH 'Acrise, Swingfield'

13 After 100 m (yd) leave tarmac and turn L across field beneath telephone lines. At the edge of field with gate ahead turn L on track between hedge and fence. Pass underneath telephone lines aiming towards farm and gate at far end of field

14 At road R follow ing signs for Acrise

15 At T-j R 'Acrise, Swingfield', then 1st L by triangle of grass 'Swingfield, Lydden'

16 At bottom of hill, on sharp RH bend, L 'Ladwood, Henbury'

17 At T-j SA 'Rakeshole Farm'

18 From tarmac to track to earth to track and back to tarmac. At road R

19 At A260 L 'Can terbury', then 1st R 'Wootton' to return to start

Behind the White Cliffs: the North Downs near Dover

Starting from the centre of Dover, the ride climbs steeply via the North Downs Way, crossing the A2 as it continues northwards along leafy tracks. The route swings south into and out of the steep valley in which Dover is situated. A stiff challenge faces the fit and those who are determined not to get off on the climb up from Kearnsey to Ewell Minnis. A pub awaits you in Ewell Minnis if you need sustenance. Through Alkham and a steep climb on the road leaves you at the top of the Downs, with a long descent along farm tracks, then through an industrial estate to return to Dover.

 Start

The Old Gaol in the centre of Dover

🅿 Follow signs

 Distance and grade

26 km (16 miles)

🥾🥾🥾 Moderate

 Terrain

Three climbs, one of 122 m (400 ft) from Dover to the A2, one of 100 m (330 ft) from Temple Ewell to Ewell Minnis and the last from Alkham to the top of the Downs

 Nearest railway

Dover

 Refreshments

Lots of choice in **Dover**
Fox PH, **Temple Ewell**
New Castle Inn, **Ewell Minnis**
Marquis of Granby PH, **Alkham**

Pineham

120
100
80
130
20
0
5
10

Dover Castle 1

Dover Castle is one of the largest and best preserved castles in England and has the longest recorded history of any fortress in England. It is thought to have been part of an Iron Age hill fort and there are Roman, medieval, Georgian and Victorian remains. In the grounds is the Roman lighthouse, the Pharos, the tallest surviving roman structure in Britain. The keep, curtain walls and outer fortifications were built in the 12th century and it was strengthened again in the 13th. It was changed greatly during the Napoleonic Wars when many of the towers had their tops cut off to provide artillery platforms. Most of the castle is open to the public and there are excellent views over the English Channel from the battlements. The secret tunnels and war headquarters of Vice-Admiral Ramsay can be toured at Hellfire Corner.

The White Cliffs Experience and the Dover Museum

This 'museum' brings the history of Dover alive with audio-visual shows, talking exhibits and even an old ferry deck that can make you feel sea sick. Next door is the Dover Museum, which houses original artefacts from prehistoric times up to the present day.

Dover Old Town Gaol

Audio-visual techniques take you back to Victorian times to hear the stories of the prisoners and gaolers. The courtroom, cells, exercise yard and bathroom have been reconstructed.

Alkham

130   140   90

15   20   26

1 From the Old Gaol R on Ladywell. At traffic lights diagonally L onto Park Avenue

2 At T-j with Connaught Road L, then just before T-j with Barton Road R by the Primary School up Old Charlton Road

3 Just past St Edmunds Catholic School on your left, L onto Roman Road 'North Downs Way'

4 At fork at end of tarmac R 'Byway. North Downs Way'. When you reach the busy A2, keep following the North Downs Way.

5 At road L (in effect SA). Just after passing triangle of grass, with no through road by a white house on your right, R onto track 'Byway'

6 At next road SA 'Byway' across field towards wood then bear R along edge of wood. Follow in same direction to road

7 At road L, following signs for Whitfield

8 At X-roads with A256 SA onto Nursery Lane

9 At T-j with Singledge Lane R 'Shepherdswell, Coldred'

10 Shortly after Longfield Farm and caravan park on your right next left on no through road 'Public Bridleway'

11 L on track before farm, following main track over field, under A2 and immediately L through double metal gates to gate in far left hand corner of field (may be rough/muddy)

12 From gate bear R down through field towards wood and red-brick houses in the valley

13 Good descent to road. At road SA 'Alkham 3. To the church'

14 Under railway bridge. At T-j with Alkham Road (B2060) R, then immediately R on tarmac 'Bridleway'

15 Tough challenge to cycle up this hill! Follow tarmac/track/ single track in same direction (may be rough/muddy). At edge of wood follow RH field edge to next blue arrow on white sign

16 Follow for almost 1½ km (1 mile). Take 1st tarmac lane on L by house. Past New Castle Inn. At T-j with road by telephone box L then R 'Public Bridleway'

17 Through wood, across field. At road R then L 'Hougham 2, Capel 2½'

18 Steep climb. At X-roads L 'St Radigund's 1¾, River 2½'

19 On sharp LH bend by barns R (in effect SA) onto track

20 Through farm, down road past industrial estate. At roundabout SA onto Coombe Valley Road

21 At X-roads with main road R, following one-way system and signs for town centre (follow Cherry Tree Avenue, Barton Road, Frith Road, Charlton Green Road), then opposite Job Centre get into RH lane and follow signs for police station to return to the start

Useful addresses

British Cycling Federation
National Cycling Centre
Stuart Street
Manchester M11 4DQ
0870 871 2000
www.bcf.uk.com

The BCF co-ordinates and promotes an array of cycle sports and cycling in general. They are a good first point of contact if you want to find out more about how to get involved in cycling. The website provides information on upcoming cycle events and competitions.

CTC (Cyclists Touring Club)
Cotterell House
69 Meadrow
Godalming
Surrey GU7 3HS
01483 417217
www.ctc.org.uk

Britain's largest cycling organisation, promoting recreational and utility cycling. The CTC provides touring and technical advice, legal aid and insurance, and campaigns to improve facilities and opportunities for all cyclists. The website provides details of campaigns and routes and has an online application form.

The London Cycling Campaign
Unit 228
30 Great Guildford Street
London SE1 0HS
020 7928 7220
www.lcc.org.uk

The LCC promotes cycling in London by providing services for cyclists and by campaigning for more facilities for cyclists. Membership of the LCC provides the following benefits: London Cyclist magazine, insurance, legal advice, workshops, organised rides, discounts in bike shops and much more. You can join the LCC on its website.

Sustrans
Head Office
Crown House
37-41 Prince Street
Bristol BS1 4PS
General information line: 0117 929 0888
www.sustrans.org.uk

A registered charity, Sustrans designs and builds systems for sustainable transport. It is best known for its transformation of old railway lines into safe, traffic-free routes for cyclists and pedestrians and wheelchair users. Sustrans is developing the 13,000 km (8000 mile) National Cycle Network on traffic-calmed minor roads and traffic-free paths, to be completed by the year 2005 with major funding from the Millennium Commission.

Veteran Cycle Club
Membership Secretary
31 Yorke Road
Croxley Green
Rickmansworth
Herts WD3 3DW
www.v-cc.org.uk

A very active club, the VCC is concerned with the history and restoration of veteran cycles. Members enjoy organised rides and receive excellent publications relating to cycle history and club news.